Continuity in Administrative Science

Ancestral Books in the Management of Organizations

A 31-volume facsimile series
reproducing classic works in the field.

Edited by
Arthur P. Brief
Graduate School of Business Administration
New York University

A Garland Series

Social Science Approaches to Business Behavior

Chris Argyris, Robert Dubin, Mason Haire, R. Duncan Luce, W. Lloyd Warner, William Foote Whyte

George B. Strother, editor

Garland Publishing, Inc.
New York • London
1987

For a complete list of the titles in this series
see the final pages of this volume

This facsimile has been made from a copy
in the Yale University Library.

© 1962 by Richard D. Irwin, Inc.
Reprinted by permission of The Dorsey Press.

Library of Congress Cataloging-in-Publication Data

Social science approaches to business behavior.

(Continuity in administrative science)
Reprint. Originally published: Homewood, Ill. :
Dorsey Press : R.D. Irwin, 1962.
(Irwin-Dorsey series in behavioral science in business)
1. Organizational behavior. I. Argyris, Chris, 1923- . II. Series.
HD58.7.S66   1987   658.4   86-25802
ISBN 0-8240-8201-X   (alk. paper)

The volumes in this series are printed on
acid-free, 250-year-life paper.

Printed in the United States of America

Social

Science

Approaches

to Business

Behavior

THE IRWIN-DORSEY SERIES IN BEHAVIORAL SCIENCE IN BUSINESS

EDITORIAL COMMITTEE

JOHN F. MEE   DONALD W. TAYLOR   WILLIAM FOOTE WHYTE
Indiana University   *Yale University*   *Cornell University*

ARGYRIS, DUBIN, HAIRE, LUCE, WARNER, WHYTE, & STROTHER (ed.)
Social Science Approaches to Business Behavior

GUEST *Organizational Change: The Effect of Successful Leadership*

LAWRENCE, BAILEY, KATZ, SEILER, ORTH, CLARK, BARNES, & TURNER
Organizational Behavior and Administration: Cases, Concepts, and Research Findings

RUBENSTEIN & HABERSTROH (eds.) *Some Theories of Organization*

WHYTE *Men at Work*

Social

Science

Approaches

to Business

Behavior

CHRIS ARGYRIS
Yale University

ROBERT DUBIN
University of Oregon

MASON HAIRE
University of California

R. DUNCAN LUCE
University of Pennsylvania

W. LLOYD WARNER
Michigan State University

WILLIAM FOOTE WHYTE
Cornell University

GEORGE B. STROTHER, *editor*
University of Wisconsin

1962
Homewood, Illinois
The Dorsey Press, Inc., *and* Richard D. Irwin, Inc.

First Printing, January, 1962

Library of Congress Catalogue Card No. 62–11285

PRINTED IN THE UNITED STATES OF AMERICA

FOREWORD

Dᴜʀɪɴɢ recent years scholars and businessmen have become increasingly aware of the fact that management decisions are influenced by a host of noneconomic factors as well as the traditional economic ones. Business schools have been exploring ways in which the research findings and methods of the behavioral sciences and mathematical statistics can be brought to bear on the managerial decision-making process. A major problem in synthesizing the approaches of economics, mathematics, and social science is that these academic disciplines have developed somewhat in isolation from each other. Consequently, their interactions can be brought about only through conscious and very carefully planned action.

The Ford Foundation with foresight has given impetus to the interdisciplinary approach to business problems by making grants to selected schools of business administration for the purpose of bringing scholars from related fields to stimulate and broaden the thinking of business school staff members, their colleagues in the university, and the business community. The University of Wisconsin School of Commerce received one of these Ford Foundation grants in recognition of a long-standing interest in this field and with a view to its further development.

The men whose contributions appear in this book each spent a period of time on the University of Wisconsin campus and, in addition to lecturing, spent many hours with faculty and graduate students exploring the theories and methods of interdisciplinary research. The faculty of the School of Commerce desire me to express their thanks, both to the scholars and to the Ford Foundation, for this enriching experience. We believe that the readers will get some of the same enthusiasm and interest that we derived from our association with the contributors. There is hope, also, that those interested primarily in other disciplines will find possibilities of research interest in business problems.

I should also like to acknowledge the productive effort of Professors W. Beranek, J. C. Schabacker, G. B. Strother, E. E. Werner, and H. D. Wolfe who served as a faculty committee which planned and conducted the Ford Foundation's program.

E. A. GAUMNITZ
Dean, School of Commerce
The University of Wisconsin

CONTENTS

Introduction

CHANGING CONCEPTS
OF TEACHING AND RESEARCH
IN BUSINESS

George B. Strother

"In the sweat of thy face shalt thou eat bread" was the ultimate of the dire punishments levied against man as penalty for original sin. By opposition, freedom from work has been regarded in most societies, civilized and primitive, as the mark of the elect. Modern students of society have frequently glossed over this fact. In attributing the evils of work to industrialization, they forget that Adam and the man with the hoe were farmers.

But if work has been regarded with aversion or, at best, with ambivalence since earliest recorded times, industrialization and the rise of the bureaucratic mechanism of control have given new meanings to the enduring conflict. One of the major differences between modern and ancient attitudes toward work arises from the fact that the management of work and commerce, which was once the job of a carefully selected group of serfs or slaves, has now become the function of a middle class whose ultimate reward is membership in the upper or leisure class. In America, in particular, Poor Richard, the Horatio Alger legend, and the Protestant ethic have glorified the rewards of industry and the moral values it confers. But, as with the Norse warrior of old, the reward is not in the act it-

1

self but in the Valhalla where the good warrior enjoys his leisure.

Frontier America in the days of the mining camp dreamed of the big strike and at the same time poked fun at the *nouveau riche* who made it. Bret Harte's heroines and heroes, pinched by their corsets and boiled shirts, expressed the national sour grapes toward others' business and financial success. Sinclair Lewis and Scott Fitzgerald in the twenties culminated this series of social critics and enriched the language with new epithets.

In more recent years the lively arts of caricature and satire have been replaced by a dreary semiscientific series of "exposés" in which the organization man, the hidden persuader, and the captive social scientist are dissected for the edification of an upper-middlebrow public. The spirit of the times changes, but the underlying attitudes remain the same. Work and the organization of work in industry, finance, and commerce are regarded as a necessary evil on the way to a Valhalla where the fruits of virtue are enjoyed without restraint. The underlying assumption that work is good only as it leads to a state of nonwork and that useful effort represents a lower form of activity than nonuseful effort can be better understood in considering not only work but also education for work. Thorstein Veblen's essay on the higher learning[1] reasons that the persistence of dead languages in the curriculum (in preference to other, more fruitful studies) can be explained only by their uselessness and their consequent value as a form of conspicuous consumption.

Veblen indulged in a deliberate *reductio ad absurdum* of his position, but, at the other extreme, it is not so clear that the Hutchins-Adler–Great Books *reductio* results from any such conscious overstatement. On the contrary, the neoscholastic revival is a deliberate protest against the application of a utilitarian yardstick in higher education.

The absurdity of this position stems from a transformation of

---

[1] *The Theory of the Leisure Class.*

values. Virtue is seen to inhere in the subject of inquiry rather than in the spirit and method. By such a transformation, scholasticism substituted the study of Aristotle for the study of nature and the study of syntax for the study of living language. In more recent times the persistence of Euclid's geometry in the high schools despite major changes in mathematical thought and the tenacity of the "mental discipline" argument for the Latinized approach to foreign languages indicate that the belief in the immanent virtue of certain subject-matter areas dies hard.

The argument that a subject should be taught because it is immediately useful seems to carry decreasing weight as one moves from the lower grades into the secondary and collegiate levels. It may be coincidence that this change is correlated with a rising level of socioeconomic selectivity, but the association at the collegiate level also appears to be correlated with the socioeconomic selectivity of the institution itself. In general, the more "exclusive" colleges place more emphasis on the purely cultural subjects and minimize the teaching of utilitarian subjects.

This disagreement as to the proper goals of higher education has taken on added focus for those concerned with collegiate business education following the publication of a number of critical studies and articles on collegiate schools of business. These reports have generally agreed in pointing out a number of defects in current business education. The authors' hope, no doubt, was that these reports might do for schools of business what the Flexner report did years ago for the medical schools.

The parallels between the poorer medical schools at the turn of the century and the poorer schools of business today arise from problems in common: caliber of students, curriculum, methods of teaching, and attitudes of the staffs of the schools. The cause-and-effect relationships are less clear, however, in the case of modern schools of business. Have poor teaching and impoverished curricula attracted poor students, or have poor students attracted poor teachers and produced impoverished curricula? One interpretation that has received little attention is that the problem starts from none of these sources but that the general position of schools of business arises from the prevailing cultural attitude toward business. Even in schools of business where academic standards are high and the average caliber of student equal to or above that of the corresponding liberal arts college, there is some indication that the business school maintains this position not by attracting the best minds but by excluding the worst. Since socioeconomic status is highly correlated with academic ability, these facts suggest that an unfavorable cultural attitude toward the study of the useful arts may be responsible for the caliber of students whom business schools attract.

The remedy which a majority of critics of business education seem to favor is to increase the amount of liberal education in the business curriculum possibly to the point where all business courses will be offered at the graduate level. A second favored remedy appears to be to change the course content from a vocational skill to a decision-making and problem-solving approach. Other remedies, not necessarily mutually exclusive, include more emphasis on quantitative approaches, more emphasis on abstraction and less on description, and the use of cases as the primary or sole teaching device. The peculiar virtues claimed by some of the adherents of these approaches appear to rest on a belief that there is only one road to salvation.

There has been little disposition by critics to consider all alternatives. Logically, there are at least three possibilities which might be pursued.

First, the study of business could be stripped of all immediately useful aims and studied as knowledge-for-its-own-sake. The commerce of the Phoenicians and the Sumerians would then be proper objects of inquiry, but the commerce of America in the 1960's would await the hallowing of time.

Second, business education could be treated as preparation for work, with an emphasis on job knowledge or job skills. The question then arises as to whether this is the proper scope of colleges and universities. The record of schools of engineering, medicine, and law argue the acceptability of this approach. There appear, on the other hand, to be some who feel that business education should be treated as subcollegiate and taught by vocational schools for those whose endowment or circumstances preclude a truly higher education. In medicine, law, and engineering the emphasis on basic knowledge and the exacting level of vocational skills involved have ruled out any serious consideration of this subcollegiate approach. In nursing, accounting, the ministry, and such trades as embalming, both approaches are used. The arbitrary exclusion of this possibility for business suggests that the study of business and conspicuous leisure are especially incompatible.

The third possibility is that business education could be regarded as a form of liberal education in the same way as the natural sciences and the humanities. There seems to be no generally accepted definition of a liberal education to aid in appraising this approach. The emphasis in liberal education has historically been on the traditional subject-matter areas. However, a look back through the years at these areas as listed in college catalogues will reveal great changes both in content and in emphasis. These shifts serve as a reminder that a discipline in the original sense of the word referred only to a group of pupils gathered under one master. The traditional disciplines are the result of a series of historical accidents. All were once philosophy, and philosophy begat rhetoric and natural philosophy and political economy and so on.

In recent years these traditional lines have fortunately become blurred. The mathematician and the astronomer, the physicist and the chemist, the psychologist and the sociologist wander more freely in a no-man's land of events which yield sometimes to one approach and sometimes to another. The picture is further complicated by the programs of general studies or general education of the forties and fifties and the interdisciplinary studies programs of the fifties and the sixties. A course entitled "Introduction to the Natural Sciences" may be taught by physicist, chemist, or biologist. A major in Latin-American studies will include courses in geography, history, literature, government, and economics. Even at the doctoral level, disciplinary boundaries are crossed and recrossed as scholars leave and return to the traditional subject-matter fields.

There is nothing inherently unhealthy about all this inter-breeding. It supports the hypothesis that there is no such thing as an orthodox liberal education. Heterodoxy is characteristic, and hybrid vigor may result as naturally as inter-species sterility. In fact, it is this heterodoxy coupled with a certain spirit and method of inquiry that probably separates the liberal from the restrictive approach to learning. If this is true, then liberal arts colleges have no monopoly on liberal educa-tion. They may indeed harbor some highly illiberal educators, drillmasters and hairsplitters whose only claim to distinction is the esotericness of the knowledge they profess.

This tendency to distinguish higher and lower forms of in-tellectual activity on a utilitarian basis carries over to the dis-tinction between pure and applied science. The history of thought is replete with examples of men who were undisturbed by the compulsion to distinguish between pure and applied studies—Archimedes, Francis Bacon, Ben Franklin, and Enrico Fermi, to mention a few. Men of this sort may be equally at home in a department of biology or a school of medicine, a de-partment of physics or a college of engineering, as long as freedom of inquiry exists. Applied studies have led to basic dis-coveries, and basic research has led to immediate applica-tions. These observations suggest that there may be little to choose from in regarding the best of collegiate business educa-tion either as high-level vocational education or as liberal edu-cation; if there is a choice to be made, it must be in how these two approaches are balanced against each other. An excess of emphasis on the immediately vocational function of business schools is a product of their origin by fission from departments of economics. The emphasis has thus been on the applications of economics to problems of business, and in the best of the schools so oriented the high-level vocational education ap-proach has predominated. The Wharton School of Finance at the University of Pennsylvania, the first school of business in the nation, exemplified this approach. Harvard, on the other hand, pre-eminent in the field of liberal education, in emphasizing problem-solving approaches to specific cases, was one of the first to recruit faculty from a variety of disciplines. But neither of these two schools nor any other few can be said to have shaped the course of modern approaches to business education as much as events outside schools of business. Despite the vague feeling that it is more respectable academically to study labor than business or the industry of Babylon than that of Gary, Indiana, an increasing number of able social scientists have become interested in the study of modern business.

The trend started early in psychology. The Leipzig laboratory of Wilhelm Wundt—the first experimental psychological laboratory in the world—was the training ground of a majority of Europe's and America's first-generation psychologists. Among the ablest of this group was Hugo Muensterberg. Unconventional and imaginative, Muensterberg abandoned traditional experimental psychology after coming to the United States in 1892. During his professorship at Harvard, his studies in legal psychology, psychotherapy, and industrial psychology earned him the title of "father of applied psychology."

During World War I the productivity studies of the British Munitions Board and the testing program of the United States Army further focused attention on the applications of psychology to personnel selection and management. Meanwhile, the ideas of Taylor and the Gilbreths had gained wide acceptance in industry, and, although, of the three, only Lillian Gilbreth was a psychologist, it was in psychology as much as any field that the concepts of human engineering were developed. The work of some sociologists and anthropologists during this era was only tangentially related to the problems of business and industry, but the direct involvement of social scientists was primarily in the field of psychological studies.

The studies of the World War I era and the twenties centered primarily around an input-output approach to the human problems of industry. The human being was regarded largely as an isolated phenomenon affected by a variety of environmental conditions which could increase or decrease his output. Elton Mayo's account of the Hawthorne studies seems to indicate that these studies, too, were undertaken with a human engineering orientation. But it is probably significant that the members of the research group at Hawthorne were sociologically oriented, so that their interpretation of their results emphasized the social factors in production. The door was thus thrown open for a more direct involvement of the sociologist and the anthropologist in the study of business and industry.

If the 1920's could be called the era of the human engineering approach, the 1930's marked the beginning of the human relations approach. The jurisdictional lines between the social sciences have become increasingly blurred as a result of this approach. Psychologists use the methods of sociology and write like sociologists, anthropologists use methods traditionally associated with psychology and draw psychological conclusions. A reader unfamiliar with the history of the authors of this book would find it difficult to identify the basic fields in which these writers received their training. At least one would prefer the title of social psychologist, which is to say neither exclusively sociologist nor exclusively psychologist but some of both. The work of social scientists in the field of business has become not only interdisciplinary, implying co-operation between different kinds of social scientists, but also multidisciplinary, implying the use by individual social scientists of the tools of more than one discipline.

That this integrated approach of the social sciences has been productive is amply attested by the growing volume of studies, books, and journals which combine the traditional approaches and avoid departmental labels. But new approaches beget new problems. There is certainly nothing inherently wrong with the multidisciplinary approach. The accidental nature of the traditional boundaries between subject-matter fields has already been noted. An eclectic approach at its best seeks to preserve the unity of natural phenomena. At its worst, however, an integrated approach may be merely faddish and superficial. A sociologist who dabbles in mathematics may be a poor sociologist and a worse mathematician. A survey approach may sacrifice needed depth in its effort to achieve breadth, and the joint efforts of a research team may simply attain the lowest common denominator of understanding. Textbooks made up of readings from widely varied sources can hardly achieve the integrity of individual effort.

Likewise, the effect of these developments on the education of businessmen may be either good or bad. Or it may be some of both. To the extent that the social sciences contribute only a short-run how-to-do-it approach or a mere cataloguing of facts, the results will be short-lived and of little value. To the extent, however, that the social sciences can contribute to a higher level of vocational education and to a better understanding of the principles governing the conduct of modern, large-scale enterprise and the people it comprises, the composition and outlook of schools of business can benefit substantially.

When the Ford Foundation made a grant to the University of Wisconsin's School of Commerce to explore the contribution of the social sciences to business, six visiting professors were invited. The plan was to make the association close enough and long enough that ideas, methods, research results, and points of view could be exchanged formally in the classroom and informally in the office and over the coffee cup. Six different universities were represented, spanning the continent. The backgrounds of the men themselves and their research interests were as varied as their locations: Robert Dubin of Oregon, a sociologist interested in work groups and the social organization of work; Mason Haire of California, a psychologist studying the growth of organizations; William Foote Whyte of Cornell, who might best be described as a social anthropologist concerned with human relations in the work environment; Lloyd Warner of Michigan State, an anthropologist analyzing the backgrounds and characteristics of executives in business and government; R. Duncan Luce of Pennsylvania, a mathematician and psychologist doing pioneering work in decision theory and choice behavior; and Chris Argyris of Yale, a social psychologist examining man's attitude toward his work environment.

The papers presented here do not hang together as a series

of connected reports. The relation among them lies in the way in which they illustrate the diversity and heterodoxy of the approaches that behavioral scientists are now using to study the business enterprise. The techniques range from the theoretico-experimental work in decision theory of Duncan Luce, whose connection with the world of business is, as he says, quite remote, to the trained-observer type of reporting that is characteristic of William Foote Whyte.

None of these papers represents applied research in the sense that the reader is expected to sell more soap or get more work from his employees as a result of reading them. They represent, on the contrary, examples of a more fruitful type of cooperation between the social sciences and business. Serving no ideology or narrow immediate purpose, they illustrate the meaning of a liberal business education and have vocational value only in the sense that they contribute to the understanding of the principles that govern organizations and men at work. They are applied studies only in the sense that they apply to our own time and place and not to remote events. It is no belittlement of the contribution of the economists who still constitute the majority of the faculties of schools of business to say that these men recruited from the behavioral sciences are products and producers of a revolution in our approach to a better understanding of business. Their extension of the educational base of schools of business prophesies an increasing recognition of business education as a broad-gauged and exacting preparation for intellectual and social fulfillment. Presently useful activity seen in this widening perspective is losing the stigma of original sin.

1

BUSINESS BEHAVIOR
BEHAVIORALLY VIEWED

Robert Dubin

SUPPOSE we take a good sample of studies of organizational behavior by behavioral scientists or those researchers who use behavioral science methods. Suppose we then extract the *behaviors* of executive and administrative personnel as reported in these studies.[1] Will these data improve our understanding of managerial *actions?*

It is the task of this chapter to attempt an answer to this question. We shall focus attention on the business institution. Occasionally studies of administrative action in other institutional settings will be examined if they shed light on what happens in administering business firms. It is not our purpose to say something about *all* administrative behavior; this we leave for general treatises and philosophical analyses.[2] Indeed, it

---

[1] We shall specifically exclude studies of *attitudes* of managers or subordinates' reactions to them. If behavioral science means what it says, then behavior and the situations of behavior must be the first levels of analysis. The sociologist W. I. Thomas, whose dictum, "If men define situations as real, they are real in their consequences," gave to social scientists their license to study attitudes, almost to the exclusion of looking at behavior. It has now become so fashionable to count, measure, and interpret attitudes that behavioral studies are difficult to find in the literature on administration, as well as in many other fields of behavioral science.

[2] Such as Herbert A. Simon, *Administrative Behavior* (New York: Macmillan Co., 1947), and Chester I. Barnard, *The Functions of the Executive* (Cambridge: Harvard University Press, 1938).

would not be possible to cover all administrative behavior, because there are many aspects that have never been behaviorally studied.

Beginnings have to be made. March and Simon[3] have essayed a heroic assemblage of propositions with data of varying quality marshaled in their support. These propositions have order and plausibility because the authors were good model builders and not because the data were available to test each proposition adequately (or even any of them well). I have chosen a different tactic. It is my intention to start from good descriptive data and discuss generalizations that can be arrived at inductively.

MANAGERIAL BEHAVIORS

It is one of the curiosities of the literature on managerial behavior that we know almost nothing about it in any detail. Even such simple facts as the kinds of activities that managers engage in and the time distributions among them are not a matter of general knowledge in the literature. We can quote the plant manager cited by Guest (33),[*] who says: "You know, I'd like to know what a foreman does, what he *really* does."

It is the purpose of this section of our analysis to assemble the data now available to answer this question for executives and foremen. The data are remarkably sparse and yet contain some surprises by way of departure from current beliefs about managers. We shall start with executives.

The simplest and most obvious fact about executives is revealed by an account of their activities and interactions. Burns, in studying four departmental executives in an English factory (12), showed that, in 80 per cent of all the time spent by these executives at work, they were *talking*. Carlson (13, p. 27) reported a 1949 study of 12 German industrial "directors" (top operating executives) who averaged 70 per cent of their time talking. Stogdill and Shartle (56, author's letter sup-

---

[3] *Organizations* (New York: John Wiley & Sons, 1958).

[*] Numbers in parentheses refer to the bibliography at the end of the chapter.

plementing publication) found that a sample of 470 Navy officers estimated that they spent 59.6 per cent of their time in contact with persons. Ulrich, Booz, and Lawrence (58), in their study of an American factory by observational methods, concluded that ". . . a rough estimate might be made that 50 to 60 per cent of a department head's time was spent in talking to men from outside the immediate ranks of his own subordinates." That, of course, did not include the additional time he spent in discourse with his own people. Fox (30) cited Kriesberg and Guetzkow as reporting for a large sample of executives that the businessmen estimated that they spent between one fourth and one half of their time in conferences.

Perhaps the sheer investment in talking time accounts for one of Carlson's minor findings (13, p. 83) that there were chief executives who signed not more than one or two letters a week, with the maximum two or three letters a day. Written communication simply does not have a chance when oral communication demands so much of the executive's time.

Is it any wonder, then, that in any catalogue of executive abilities it seems clear why "ability to express himself" is a leading one? In the sheer volume of all activities demanded of him, verbal interaction is the No. 1 form of contact, consuming upward of 80 per cent of all the executive's time. Bendix (8) has argued that the so-called human relations movement was a response to the need for a new managerial justification for the exercise of authority with the passing of the owner-entrepreneur and his replacement by the professional, salaried executive. He cited Dale Carnegie as the principal evangelist of this movement. But perhaps a simpler, less elegant, more realistic interpretation of the movement to "win friends and influence people" through verbal skills is to consider it a simple response to the behavioral demands of the executive role—the executive simply spends so much of his time talking that he has to be skillful at it in order to succeed.

As if to emphasize the other side of the coin of "togetherness," Carlson has some fascinating data on "aloneness" for a single top Swedish executive (13, pp. 72–73). The observational data showed that the average length of time that the executive was alone was only 14 minutes for a given period. If uninterrupted time alone (undisturbed by visitors and telephone calls) was considered, then this averaged only 8 minutes per alone period. Indeed, only 12 times in 35 days of observation was this chief executive able to work undisturbed alone in his office during intervals of 23 minutes or longer. Dale (20) reported in a general way a recurrent complaint by American executives that they lacked the opportunity for time to be alone and uninterrupted.

We start, then, with a picture of the executive scarcely able to close his mouth, with an extremely high proportion of his time spent in discourse with others in his environment. Assuming that he wanted to have time alone to think, read, relax, or even dream big for the company's future, the one study we have of a single executive in action reveals that there is pitifully little time to do this.[4]

With whom is this vast expenditure of time spent by executives in interacting with other people in the organization? Our data shift to middle managers, for, unfortunately, there are no data known to me dealing with top management. Rearranging Burns's facts about his four departmental managers, we secure the picture presented in Table 1. This table shows the dis-

TABLE 1

PER CENT OF EXECUTIVES' TOTAL INTERACTION TIME SPENT
WITH PEOPLE OF VARIOUS RANKS

Ranking of Person with Whom Interacting	Department Manager	His Senior Staff*	His Junior Staff†
Superiors	6	23	34
Peers	29	50	46
Subordinates	65	27	20

Source: Burns (12, p. 90) observational data.
* Comparable to assistant departmental manager (actually one person).
† Comparable to section manager with foremen under him.

_____

[4] I am willing to bet that there will even be executives who will have the contents of this book "briefed," so that they may benefit without burdening themselves with reading the entire contents in the scraps of reading time available to them!

tribution of time spent in contact with others and, of course, does not include time spent alone. Two notable features of the data call for comment.

First, as we go downward in rank, the proportion of time spent with superiors markedly increases, and, correspondingly, the proportion of time spent with subordinates decreases. That is to say, in the lower reaches of management more time is spent looking upward than downward in the rank system. This again accords with general observations (Roethlisberger [52]; Dubin [26, pp. 373–75]), but it is especially comforting to have actual data that substantially support the impressionistic observational conclusion. This conclusion, incidentally, helps to orient the data on foremen which we shall examine shortly.

Second, we observe that there is a very substantial increase in the proportion of time spent in interaction that is devoted to peers as we move downward in the rank system. This reaches half the total interacting time for the senior and junior staff men under the departmental manager. Now there is almost no notice taken in the literature (good *exceptions* being Richardson and Walker [51, pp. 55–85] and the anecdotal accounts of Dalton [23]) of the *horizontal* dimension of organization and the volume of business that is transacted among *peers* to keep the organization going. Indeed, it is probably among organizational equals that much of the real co-ordination of work flow and operations takes place in what Dubin has called the "nonformal behavior system" (28, chap. 4). The nonformal behavior system is the arena in which the organization is made to work by supplementing the formal procedures, rules, etc., with realistic applications of them to operating situations. Jaques pointed to nonformal behavior systems when he concluded from his long-term observational study of the English factory (35, p. 270) that ". . . it is an impossible task to make policy completely explicit. There remains always a residue of unrecognized and unidentified aspects of the culture of the concern. . . . The identification and labelling of these is a never-ending process." Weiss (59, p. 62) gives some brief descriptions of nonformal behavior among government research administrators, although not labeling it by this term.

It cannot be too strongly emphasized that horizontal relations among peers in management and the nonformal behavior systems through which such interactions are carried out constitute a dimension of organizational behavior long neglected and probably as important as authority relations. We shall see this same characteristic peer-to-peer interaction as an important form of contact among foremen in doing their work.

The mode of interaction up and down the ranks of management is revealed by examining the initiation of contacts. Again our hard data are meager, and we return to Burns's study. (Illustrative data are abundant in the work of Whyte [60] and Argyris [3], but it is impossible to do more than accept their conclusions as plausible, since no distributions of data are presented by these investigators.) In Table 2 we have the dis-

TABLE 2

INITIATION OF INTERACTION BY A DEPARTMENTAL MANAGER

Interactions with—	Total Interactions Recorded	Per Cent Initiated by Manager
Superiors	41	36
Peers	183	51
Subordinates		
Senior staff	402	58
Design-planning staff, foremen	154	62
Working supervisors, senior clerical, etc.	27	74
Apprentices, typists, etc.	63	62

Source: Burns (12, p. 90).

tribution of 870 recorded interactions of the departmental manager showing the proportion of each class of interaction which he initiated. It is notable that this one man initiated exactly half the interactions with his peers, much more than half and up to three quarters for his subordinates, and only about a third to his superiors. We seem to have confirmed here an inverse law of initiation of interaction in which the proportion of initiation increases from high to low rank, the greater the difference in rank between initiator and recipient.

Our next concern is to ask "What are principal areas of functional responsibility of executives?" The data from two studies are presented in Table 3. The Stogdill-Shartle study reports

TABLE 3

PER CENT OF EXECUTIVES' TIME SPENT IN AREAS OF FUNCTIONAL BEHAVIOR

Area of Functional Behavior	470 Navy Officers*	66 Wholesale Co-operative Executives*	Swedish Managing Directors, Centralized Organizations	Swedish Managing Directors, Decentralized Organizations
Getting information	18	18	37.9	39.6
Advising and explaining	13	12	15.9	14.6
Making decisions	28	26	14.6	6.3
Giving orders	15	15	13.8	6.8
Others	26	29	17.8	32.7
Data-gathering method	Self-estimate	Self-estimate	Observation	Observation
Source	Stogdill-Shartle (56, p. 49)	Stogdill-Shartle (56, p. 49)	Carlson (13)	Carlson (13)

* Combination of reported categories.

self-estimate data, while Carlson's data are based on observational records.[5] There may be other data of this sort, but we were not able to uncover it readily.[6]

The most outstanding (if not startling) fact presented by the table is the small proportion of time spent on making decisions.[7] If these studies are at all representative of what execu-

[5] In considering these data, it should be kept in mind that there may be real differences between observation of action and self-estimates of it. Burns (12), who did actual observational studies of executives and who also asked them to estimate their own time spent in activities, showed that there were significant discrepancies between the two methods of collecting the data.

[6] For example, Sayles and Chapple (54) reported the distribution of time spent by two superintendents without any reference to comparable studies. Their data are not included here because it is used by them illustratively rather than as a body of fact and is difficult to interpret for that reason.

[7] Here the observational data reported a relatively small proportion of time spent in making decisions, while the self-estimated figures reached an average of more than a quarter of the time. Does this mean that there may be some self-inflation of importance when executives evaluate their own work?

tives do, it would seem that making decisions, which is often considered their cardinal function, occupies a remarkably small share of their total working time. Perhaps these samples of executives have learned what Barnard called the fine art of decision making—"not deciding questions that are not now pertinent, in not deciding prematurely, in not making decisions that cannot be made effective, and in not making decisions that others should make."

As if to support Barnard's conclusion by indicating how much preparation goes into decision making, the observational studies of the Swedish top executives showed that they spend between a third and two fifths of their time getting information about their organizations, while the self-estimating Naval officers and American wholesale co-operative executives had to invest a major share of their time in simply getting information, suggesting (A) that they may be genuinely isolated from their organization (an often-made observation, see Drucker's study of General Motors [25], for example), this heavy investment in getting information being necessary in order to help overcome this isolation; and (B) that executives may be particular victims of dependency on flows of information within their organizations such that their decisions may be readily affected by what is fed to them, or withheld, by subordinates. Still another feature of Table 3 is the combined proportion of time spent in "giving orders" and "advising or explaining." For centralized organizations, including one group of Swedish companies, the Navy, and the wholesale co-operatives, explaining or ordering consumed about 28 per cent of an executive's time, while in the one example of decentralized organization (again Swedish data) these activities commanded only 20 per cent of the executive's time, the difference being entirely accounted for by the lesser amount of time devoted to giving orders under decentralization.

One of the curiosities of job descriptions is that they give the impression that the described components of the job are all brought into use at the same time or at least in closely connected bundles. This simple fact alone may have been important in leading academic investigators to assume that variety is a scarce commodity in business behavior and that, being the spice of life, its scarcity must thereby lead to charactcrizing the business world as tasteless and monotonous. Returning to Burns's data (12, p. 81), he showed that over a 5-week period there was significant variety in the business life of executives due to different "mixes" of the same content of their work through time.[8] As if to give added support to this idea from quite a tangential field of administration, Weiss (59, pp. 15–17) showed that the self-described bundles of activities of research administrators in a governmental research agency varied considerably among men holding identical job classifications and organizational positions. Furthermore, he showed that these bundles tended to change through time when he compared the bundles of functions claimed by men of different lengths of tenure in the same kinds of administrative positions. Both these findings strongly suggest that there may be a rhythm of "content mix" comparable to that of business executives.

One final feature of the behavior of executives deserves notice because of its linkage with a popular claim that decentralization of management not only relieves top management of operating decision-making responsibility but also, by implication, makes the total job of top managers easier. It is easy to assume that there will be less work for top executives to handle if they shift some of their work to lower levels of management (incidentally also improving the morale and involvement of managers, according to the claims). Melman (46), in his penetrating study of the English automobile factory, demonstrated, first, that there was very considerable delegation of genuine authority down to and including the work level. The major consequence of this was that top management turned its attention in greater and greater proportion to sales and the external problems of the firm. Management's total burden of work did not,

---

[8] A fact that I think equally characterizes the work of foremen and rank-and-file workers. It takes real talent and determined effort at work simplification and job standardization to *remove* variation in "content mix" from a job.

in fact, become lessened by delegation—it simply shifted to focus on the external problems of the organization. Janowitz and Delaney (36) pointed out this same phenomenon in a public bureaucracy where top management spent a significantly larger proportion of total time in public relations activities and maintaining contacts with external agencies, in contrast to lower-level officials, who really "ran" the organization day by day.

This secular trend in the shifting functions of the top executive group that comes with modification of internal decision making and authority is really another facet of the rhythm of "content mix" in executive positions that takes place over long time spans. Haire (34), in his studies of the temporal, structural shifts in four firms in the balance between administrative and other employees, pointed to a changing condition of the organization that can also have its direct impact on the "content mix" of executive positions.

We now turn to examine the behavior of foremen as it has been reported in the literature. Here we are no more fortunate in having data any better than that available on executives.

In contrast with the very high percentage of total time that executives spend in talking, it appears that foremen are much more likely to be doers than talkers. Ponder (50) reported observational studies of 12 "high effective" General Electric foremen, showing that they spent 56 per cent of their total time talking, while "low effective" GE foremen devoted 45 per cent of their time to conversation. Guest's study of 56 automobile assembly plant foremen (33), again an observational study, showed that the foremen averaged 46.6 per cent of their time in conversation. The Ponder study apparently counted all interaction contacts as "talking" contacts, while in the Guest study only actual talking was so counted. For all interpersonal contacts Guest reported that this accounted for 57.3 per cent of all the time of his 56 foremen, apparently a measure more comparable with Ponder's results.

It will be recalled that the farther down the ranks of management we went, the higher was the proportion of time spent with superiors relative to time spent with subordinates. When we get to the foreman level, however, the facts seem to indicate that foremen are so busy getting their work done that they do not have time to spend with their bosses. By recalculating the Ponder and Guest data, we secure the picture of Table 4,

TABLE 4

Per Cent of Foremen's Total Interaction Time Spent
with People of Various Ranks

Ranking of Person with Whom Interacting	12 "High Effective" General Electric Foremen	12 "Low Effective" General Electric Foremen	56 Automobile Assembly Plant Foremen	16 Midwest Production Department Foremen
Superiors	Not given	Not given	10	30
Subordinates	34	39	46	60
Peers	Not given	Not given	12	10
Others*	66	61	32	0
Data-gathering method	Observation	Observation	Observation	Observation
Source	Ponder (50)	Ponder (50)	Guest (33)	Piersol (49)

* Includes some superiors from other departments and areas, all the superiors in the two GE samples, and some subordinates and peers in other departments.

which is somewhat comparable to the similar table for executives. The data here are only suggestive, since the classifications were very loosely drawn by the original investigators. Nevertheless, it is clear that a significantly higher proportion of all interaction time was spent by foremen with their subordinates than was true for any but the department manager in the executive study. If we were able to add in the subordinates included among the "others" in the table, this result would be even more apparent.

Perhaps we can surmise from these comparative data that direct supervisory responsibility forces downward orientation for a boss, whether he is a department manager or a first-line foreman. On the other hand, it may be that line supervisors without a direct rank-and-file command or who perform both staff and line functions must spend more time interacting with the boss to find out what is expected and/or to be one of his informational sources and advisers. However we interpret these data, it seems clear that there are significant differences in the proportions of contact time spent with superiors, peers, and subordinates by various levels of managers.

Jasinski (37, p. 135), using a portion of the data from Guest's study of the 56 automobile assembly-line foremen, found that in one department of 11 foremen there were about 300 contacts among them in a single 8-hour day. He observed that an average of three quarters of all contacts for the average foreman were either with the foremen immediately preceding him on the line or with the one immediately succeeding him. Simpson (55), using reported contacts data and only accepting those contacts mutually reported for a group of 8 foremen (general foreman, two shift foremen, five crew foremen) on two shifts in the same department, showed that among the five crew supervisors there was a range of 43–76 per cent of all contacts among foremen that were peer contacts. These two reports tell us again the importance of the horizontal dimension of management and give us some clue as to the volume of nonformal relations involved in getting work done at the foreman level. To give some idea of how much this peer-level interaction is work-oriented, as our model of "nonformal relations" predicts, Ta-

TABLE 5

SUBJECTS OF FOREMAN-TO-FOREMAN INTERACTION

Subject	Per Cent of Interaction Time
Production	27.1
Personnel administration	13.7
Equipment and methods	3.1
Quality	35.8
Personal, nonwork	9.7
Other	10.6

Adapted from Jasinski (37, p. 135).

ble 5 summarizes Jasinski's data for the 11 foremen he observed. Only 9.7 per cent of the total interactions among foremen could be classified as personal—nonwork, as Table 5 shows. Almost 80 per cent of the total time spent together among foremen in the same department was devoted to the four clearly work-oriented subjects of production, personnel administration, equipment and materials, and quality of output.

For both the executive data and the foremen data we find substantial support for the plea that the horizontal interactional aspects of managerial behavior among peers be accorded significant attention in the research and theorizing about managerial behavior.

There do not appear to be data for foremen comparable with the facts about the functional behavior of executives presented above. Ponder (50) reported that his 12 "high effective" foremen gave orders 8 per cent of the time they were in interaction with subordinates, while the "low effective" foremen gave orders 16 per cent of the time. The "high effectives" received information 25 per cent of the time during contact with subordinates, while the "low effective" foremen were getting information 37 per cent of the time that they were with subordinates. These figures are not directly comparable with the similar ones for executives, since the foremen data were based only on interactions with subordinates, while the executive data covered all interactions. The most significant thing we can conclude from these foreman data is that getting information from rank-and-file workers is a relatively important behavior of foremen, just as getting information about the organization turned out to be an important behavior of executives. For those organizational theorists who still believe that some members of an organization can be *powerless*, these data on the dependence of all ranks of management on the upward flow of information should be a proper corrective. As a minimum, the rank-and-file, by controlling the information going to the foreman and then on upward, has significant power in its own hands.

There is only a single report on the balance of initiating contacts and receiving contacts by foremen. Guest (33, p. 483) reported that 60.3 per cent of all foremen contacts were initiated by them. Burns's data on the department manager, reported in Table 2, yield a comparable figure of managers' initiations of 57 per cent. The similiarity of the proportions may be noted, but, in the absence of any further comparisons, it is difficult to draw any meaningful conclusions from this fact.

One final fact of substantial agreement should be noted about the foremen's position. Three different studies, two of them based on direct observation and one based on self-records, indicated that the overwhelming content of the interaction of foremen with all other people was devoted to the close details of work. The four areas of production, personnel administration, equipment and methods, and quality account for between 63 and 78 per cent of all interactions. The details are shown in Table 6.

TABLE 6

PER CENT OF TOTAL TIME OF FOREMEN SPENT
IN AREAS OF OPERATING RESPONSIBILITY

Area of Operating Responsibility	12 "High Effective" General Electric Foremen	12 "Low Effective" General Electric Foremen	56 Automobile Assembly Plant Foremen	Radio Corporation of America Foremen
Production	20	40	34.5*	⎫
Personnel administration	23	12	13.2*	⎪
Equipment and methods	14	8	16.3*	⎬ 78
Quality	6	6	18.2	⎭
Other	37	34	17.8	22
Data-gathering method	Observation	Observation	Observation	Self-record
Source	Ponder (50)	Ponder (50)	Guest (33)	Zinck (61)

* Composite of reported categories.

We emerge, then, with the following summary picture of the content and ecology of managerial behavior. Decision making and giving orders—the classical functions of managers—seem to occupy a relatively minor amount of their time. At all levels of management a major investment of time is made in getting information from lower levels of the organization as a basis for knowing what is happening and presumably also as a basis for follow-up decisions and action. The environment of the executive is verbal to a high degree, diminishing in volume of time spent in conversation as we go down the ranks of management. A remarkable amount of total time is spent by all ranks of management with organizational peers, which, by inference, leads to the conclusion that much of the active co-ordination of actual work of the organization that "makes things really run" is carried out through nonformal relations.

ORGANIZATION ENVIRONMENT AS AN INFLUENCE ON BEHAVIOR

Bakke (7) has pointed to the "organization charter" as the embodiment of the purpose and meaning of organizational activities. In his study of the telephone company he found that the organization charter was symbolized by asking the members of management and employees to describe what the name of the organization stood for in their minds. The charter appeared to have these meanings for the members (in the order of frequency of mention): expressing the purpose and function of the company, its general significance, its reputation, its major policies, and as an organization identified with a larger system. Two consequences were seen to flow from the members' recognition of the organization charter and its symbolization: (A) the charter provided important incentive values for the members by identifying uniquely and concretely the organizational image to which loyalties were attached (7, pp. 168–69); and (B) the charter, when internalized, tended to support the authoritativeness of the member and hence to support the stability of the authority structure (7, p. 175).

The organizational charter is a very diffuse environmental feature of the organization. Its symbolization of the specific purpose of a business firm was of critical significance in establishing styles of leadership, as demonstrated in the study by Dill (24) of two Norwegian companies—one a clothing company, the other a light metal manufacturing company. The clothing company had a highly integrated technology, and the entire work flow was initiated by clothing orders received and

their subsequent production for specified delivery dates. All
operations were very interdependent. In this situation Dill
found a high degree of centralization of management with
very limited autonomy distributed to subordinate levels of executives. By contrast, the second company had thirteen distinctive product divisions, each of which was autonomous in
securing, handling, producing, and delivering its products. In
this second company there was significantly more autonomy
distributed among the ranks of management than in the first.
Dill established this finding by recording the decision-making
conferences of the respective managerial groups. He concluded
that the organizational environment characterized in terms of
functional division of labor and functional autonomy would affect leadership such that ". . . the amount of autonomy of
leaders' behavior was a function of four factors: (1) the ease
of formulating independent task assignments for different work
groups in the firm; (2) leaders' estimates of the probability
that action on tasks would lead to unpleasant personal consequences by producing unwanted results for the organization
or by producing conflict with other work groups; (3) the exclusiveness of each leader's control over information about
tasks or activities that he was formally responsible for; and
(4) leaders' estimates of the costs or gains associated with attempts to seek or to give advice" (24, p. 155).

While Dill established the fact that the organization charter
as a statement of social function and the corresponding internal division of labor to accomplish it affected delegation of authority, McMurry (45), in reporting the results of psychologically oriented interviews with 600 bank employees, concluded
that the static nature of banking operations was mirrored in
the undynamic and static nature of the banking employees'
outlook and reactions to their environment. Thus, either one
can argue that the "atmosphere" of banking tended to select
out appropriate personality types to fill the operating positions
of banking organizations (as McMurry does), or one can
contend that the behavior systems of work were readily learned
and were appropriate to the "atmosphere" of the organization,

irrespective of the personality structure of employees (as Dubin argues in emphasizing the central importance of behavior systems as part of the organization environment [28]).

Turning to still another feature of organizational environment as a determinant of managerial behavior, Fleishman and associates (29) found that foremen given human relations training were still impervious to its application in their supervisory behavior unless their own supervisors also practiced it. Their carefully controlled study made clear that the leadership climate of the foreman was more determined by the climate created by the foremen's supervisors than by the training that the foremen received. Thus other people as environment and especially direct bosses materially determine the behaviors to be displayed toward subordinates.

It is interesting that in the folklore of managerial literature much is made of the need for total immersion of the individual in his organization. One of the implications of this belief in total immersion is that the individual member should have high interest in all aspects of the organization. Jaques concluded from the long-term observational study of the English factory that managers and executives *insulated* themselves by being inattentive to and indifferent toward many aspects of the organization that were not central to their own functioning in it. Jaques concluded that this was functional for the expert performance of the executive and his concentration on his specific responsibilities and should not be interpreted as an index of apathy or lack of interest (35, pp. 302–3). Argyris (5) found this same phenomenon among production workes when management attempted to stir up an interest in the company as a whole, to which the production workers in effect replied "Nuts, leave us alone, we're doing our job, go do yours and leave us out of it."

Thus insulation or "adaptive segregation" (to use Jaques' happy phrase) may be one of the really necessary conditions for truly effective specialized performance in an organization. Pelz (47) found, for example, that government scientists tended to insulate themselves from central and departmental services staffs by such simple devices as using a telephone or written communication as a major means for avoiding face-to-face contacts in asking for services.

Still another aspect of the social environment of any organization is its past history as carried in the experiences and perceptions of those present members who experienced it. Jaques (35, pp. 313–14) pointed out how the past behaviors of older members of management colored their contemporary behavior, especially where there were status distinctions honored in the past that had to be defended against attack. It is not unreasonable to conclude that, where revolutionary changes in procedures, technologies, purposes, or other major features of organization are contemplated, the operations of "sweeping the rascals out" or "starting with a clean slate" may make sense, in order to sever the links with the past carried in the behaviors and outlook of those organization members who experienced it. This may sound drastic, but it seems realistic as one method of insuring reasonable "togetherness" about the new organization charter.

Moving into areas of perceptions that affect behavior, Weiss (59, p. 44), in studying research administrators in a government organization, found that those who described their own functions as a combination of policy making and implementing policy also reported that they believed that colleagues in the organization were highly supportive of them; that the organization made full use of their abilities; and that relatively little opportunity was available on the job to learn more (or perhaps this response could be interpreted as their covert way of saying that they had nothing more to learn). Thus it would appear that those who described themselves as running the organization by making its policy and then seeing that it was effectuated had a high sense of "self-realization," not necessarily because this was objectively true but because the nature of their directing position made such a belief functional in self-support against the stresses of opposition and "problems." Compare this with the report of Coates and Pellegrin (17), who asked a sample of executives to describe their own characteristics which they thought most important to their present success. These executives spoke of themselves as energetic, alert, aggressive, able to get along with and manipulate people, responsible, decisive, determined, adaptable, able to sell ideas, and get things done through groups—all of which gives the impression of high "self-realization." But when the same researchers asked career supervisors to describe the successful executives they knew, the same picture emerged from the responses with the one addition—these same supervisors were almost unanimous in eschewing any aspiration to be successful executives because they did not want the stress or "industrial suicide" that accompanied executive positions. Were these supervisors being extremely realistic in supporting the suggestion made above that an executive's sense of "self-realization" was one of his defenses against the stresses of his position? It may very well be that outlook and point of view attach to a position as part of its environment, serving to protect the position incumbent from the stresses of his job.

Still another interesting facet of perceptions as environment for behavior was Jaques' observation, arrived at through content analysis of discourse, that, in the factory he studied, executives often used bromides and clichés as a defense against the reality of conflict and discord among themselves (35, p. 317). For example, he pointed out that the belief that "if people were treated responsibly, they would behave responsibly," became a buttress for the idea that all discord and opposition was responsible and well-intentioned. This is one aspect of what Dubin has labeled "organization fictions" (26, chap. 20) and illustrates how beliefs may facilitate behavior in organizations, even though the beliefs are mythical and/or illogical.

One final and simple point about environment. It is a generally held precept in sociology that "like attracts like." This certainly seems to be borne out when examining the voluntary interactions of executives and members of management. Koontz and O'Donnell (40), in quoting from an American Institute of Management study published in 1951, reported that, for 100 executives in 10 leading corporations, "out of a total of 817 activities of these executives . . . 72 per cent were in clubs, societies and fraternities; . . . 17 per cent were in business associations. . . ." This means that 89 per cent of voluntary association choices of executives were either with other businessmen or with people who were similarly situated socially. As if to give the microcosmic picture of this, Ulrich, Booz, and Lawrence (58, p. 18) reported: "At company parties and dinners the [management] team members made an attempt to circulate early in the evening and ended up talking to their 'equals.'"

Again we find a number of individual generalizations, all grounded in some systematic observation of executive behavior. Each of these generalizations tells us something about the impact of selective features of the organizational environment on managerial behavior. It is also clear that there is no pat or simple relationship that can be generalized out of the generalizations (e.g., I find it hard to buy the widely peddled notion that leadership climate [read "environment"] can be the medicine to cure all organizational ills).

DECISION MAKING

One of the features of organization theory is its emphasis on decision making. This emphasis has turned in very formalistic directions, particularly since high-speed computers have made possible the rapid examination of the consequences of alternate decisions.

There are two simple and supplementary points I want to emphasize here. Both derive from studies of the behaviors of decision makers in operation rather than the study of simulating models of these decision-making operations. The observations are (A) that the *time scale* of decision is very much (and I want to underscore the "very much") longer than the formalistic analysis of decision making would lead one to expect and (B) that organizational decision making is fundamentally a *political process.*

Let us examine the time-scale problem first. Simon and his associates at Carnegie Institute of Technology have done some

of the major work on the formal analysis of decision making.
They have also studied the actual decisional process in business decisions. Cyert, Simon, and Trow (18) in a 1956 publication first reported the history of a decision regarding installa-
tion of electronic data processing. The fascinating aspect of
this study is that this highly rational decision about a highly
rational method in business operations was initiated in July,
1952, and the recommendation to the board of directors was
not made until the middle of February, 1956. There was an actual lapse of *three and three quarters years* before a plan was
hardened to the point where it could be presented for a "yes
or no" decision by the board of directors. Cyert, Dill, and
March (19) covered the same case again and added to it the
history of two other decisions. In one company the safety hazard of overhead cranes led to a consideration of their replacement by magnetically controlled cranes. After *two years* of in-
vestigation, discussion up and down the ranks of management,
and formulation and reformulation of proposals, there was a
committee recommendation that the cranes be replaced. After
all this very considerable work and thought and discussion,
the recommendation was turned down, and the old policy was
continued of making single replacements as individual cranes
wore out. Note that both these problems involved rather simple, single issues—and note the time scale over which each decision was under active consideration.

A classic and almost forgotten study of decision making is
Chamberlain's analysis of the internal-transfer policy decision
in a telephone company (14). The company problem was to
clarify its policy regarding employee transfers inside the company. This problem was first recognized and openly discussed
in 1926, with the first modern reconsideration of the problem
occurring in the fall of 1943, when a comprehensive, 6-month
survey was undertaken of the problem. The final policy was
printed in a company bulletin dated in the middle of February,
1945. The time lapse for the final active consideration of the
problem was *more than one year*.

The point should be clear and unmistakably established by

the data. Decisions in organizations take a great deal of time between the recognition of the problem and the decision regarding its solution. As the data clearly show, this time scale is a major dimension of decision making to which little or no attention has been paid. Furthermore, the data support the conclusion about time scale especially strongly because the decisions under study were largely single-subject, narrow problems requiring relatively few correlated decisions. Dale's survey of American companies (20) led him to point to the time scale involved in reaching decisions as a major obstacle to effective operations.

The sense of time scale is even further emphasized in Brown's report of the evolution of company philosophy at the famous Glacier company (11). Brown is the chief executive officer and in his own account shows how more than *ten years* elapsed since the company was first studied by Jaques and associates, who made specific recommendations regarding broad management policies and philosophies. Brown's recent account (1960) tells us that these philosophies and policies are *still* in the process of evolution, and much of his analysis is taken up with the descriptions of the snail-like pace at which these were suggested, analyzed, decided, internalized, and then acted out by the affected members of management.

If we shift attention to decisions involved in administering an established policy, we discover the same phenomenon of time lapse, although the scale is shorter. Baker and France (6, p. 160), in studying 135 companies, concluded that the most common practice in handling industrial relations policy interpretation decisions was for the foreman to refer the issue to the general foreman, who might refer it to the plant personnel man, who in turn might discuss it with headquarters. Even the first referral step took time, but much more time was added if the issue went beyond the general foreman.

The point ought to be clear. No realistic picture of decision making in organizations can emerge until we add the time dimension for making decisions. The *time scale* is exceedingly important as a fact of organizational decision making—at least partly because it provides the opportunity for the operation of the political factor in reaching decisions, to which we now turn.

By the "political factor" in decision making we mean that disparate interests and even conflicting interests of individuals or groups are accommodated in the decision itself. These differences first have to be searched out through discussion and analysis, the disparities among them made clear, and the points of compromise and accommodation determined. Finally, the actual decision incorporating the balance points among the interests has to be reached. These steps taken together involve political processes. We can illustrate the political features of decision making in organizations from the literature.

Melman (46), in an outstanding study of an English automobile factory, showed conclusively that a central feature of the highly decentralized production decision making involved major changes in the actual structure of management from that in the typical industrial establishment. Accompanying this structural accommodation in the ranks of management was the need for the union to assume some major decisional responsibilities not previously a part of union functions. The work groups also had to accommodate to the responsibility of greater autonomy placed on them by decentralization. All these accommodations involved political processes.

In the previously mentioned Cyert, Dill, and March study (19) the board of directors in one case suggested that at least two bidders be invited to seek the equipment contract for data-processing machines, leading the planning committee to believe that this meant the board's rejection of the single company under initial consideration. This is a beautiful exhibition of the political process at work when it was not necessary, since the board was really neutral as to choice and only wanted competitive bidding as a matter of policy. The politics of decision making is even more sharply etched in their case of a specialized product department whose future was under a cloud. The head of the department used strong pressures to confirm the continuity of his department, while other executives opposed him, using indirect, but very effective, means to influence a decision in the opposite direction that left the department in question with an uncertain future. Chamberlain (14) gives detailed accounts of the politics of reaching the employee-transfer decision in the telephone company. Marcson (44, pp. 112–15) found another aspect of the politics of decision among industrial scientists in the process of "hedging" by making only partial commitments of resources to problematic research projects, leaving a final decision open to retreat from additional commitment if success appeared doubtful or open to further support if preliminary results appeared promising.

Enough data have been marshaled to suggest some of the features of the politics of organizational decision. It should be clear that time is necessary to play politics. This suggests that the analytical problem of *time scale* is really coupled with the analytical problem of the *politics of decision*. The linkage can be expressed as follows: the greater the need to accommodate differences in a decision, the more time may be consumed in reaching the decision.

POWER

We mean by "power" something obvious and visible. Power is an attribute of a position in a system of interdependence. We would agree that a business firm is a set of interdependent jobs and positions. The fulfillment of each position contributes functions necessary to maintain the system in a viable state. Some functions are performed exclusively, while others are shared with colleagues in the organization. The functional importance of contribution to the organization and the exclusiveness with which functions are performed measure the power of each individual in the organization (Dubin [28]).

Thus power is meaningful in relation to the system in which functions are performed rather than, as it is usually viewed, as power over another person. The power over other persons may be a consequence of power over system functioning, but it is not an inevitable consequence. Thus "missile janitors" have high power at launching sites because extreme precautions need to be taken to keep pipe lines at near-absolute cleanliness to prevent misfired rockets (an estimated three fourths of misfires at Cape Canaveral were due to "dirty" pipes in the rocket systems). These missile janitors are persons of relatively high power on the launching pads because of the criticalness, i.e., importance, of the functions they perform in the system.

It is common practice in industry to plan out and actually make drawings or charts of work-flow processes, work-transfer processes, and other functional relationships. Bakke (7) has been one of the few behavioral scientists to present this kind of data to his professional colleagues. By examining the work-flow diagrams and functional position descriptions, it is possible to gain pictures of the power of each contributor to the telephone customer order-filling process that Bakke, for example, describes. The whole process constitutes a subsystem in the telephone company to which each individual makes a functional contribution. Some contributions are more important than others, and some gain in importance because they are made exclusively by a single individual. This material is illustrative of the basic nature of power in social systems, the effects of which we can now examine in the actual studies of the power acts of managers.[9]

Sayles (53, p. 63) has shown that industrial workers had their power made clear to them because of management's constant emphasis on their importance to the organization. Telling a person or group that they are important to the organization (because the work they do is skilled, critical, etc.) is one way of confirming their functional importance to the organiza-

---

[9] One of the better direct studies of power in organizations is by James D. Thompson, "Authority and Power in 'Identical' Organizations," reprinted as chapter 2 of *Comparative Studies in Administration*, ed. James D. Thompson *et al.* (Pittsburgh: University of Pittsburgh Press, 1959). Thompson studied two Air Force wings having identical formal organization and mission, both being under the same command. He found that those who were in each organization, or who knew how they operated, rated the officers who were most responsible for "getting things done" in different order for the two wings. These secondary observational data confirm the fact that the power structure of an organization may be quite different from the formal organizational structure because particular office holders may perform different functions in the same office or may perform the same functions differently.

tion. Dubin (27) has shown that industrial workers have differential preferences for the work setting, with formal organizational ties and technology being the most valued features of the work organization and informal social relations the least, suggesting that power in the organization is highly valued, even among rank-and-file workers.

One of the more obvious observations Jaques made about the existing management structure of his British factory was that the divisional managers' meeting constituted a management committee for the firm; sometimes functioned as a concealed board of directors; sometimes as an executive committee for only the London factory (one of several); and sometimes as a discussion group to consider mutual problems of the London plant with the managing director (president) (35, p. 216). It was this welter of different functions that the same group performed that was responsible for considerable confusion among group members. They had different powers over the affairs of the organization, depending on the particular capacity in which they were functioning. But they did not have fixed powers, and this was personally disturbing to them.

This highlights a feature of organizational power in which there may be separate bundles of power, possessed by single individuals, that are independent of each other. For each bundle, the power is specific, but all the bundles do not add up to a coherent whole. Thus we have the apparent paradox of power confusion without power diffusion. A number of writers have assumed that confusion about power results only from its lack of specificity. The English study makes clear that confusion can also be the consequence of lack of coherence among very specific powers possessed by individuals. This is another way of formalizing the folk saying, "A man can't wear too many hats at the same time."

Let us now turn to some of the behavioral adaptations to power relations in organizations. Sayles (53, p. 125) made clear that, among the four types of industrial work groups he delineated, the ones in which there was a high degree of technical interdependence were also the work groups in which there was

the highest amount of reciprocal attachment between supervisors and workers. Sayles is really saying that the more clearly
each participant recognized his dependence on the functional
performance of others and their dependence on him, the greater
was the probability that all felt stronger attachments for each
other. It is important to note that this mutuality of attachment
was not directly the product of "leadership climate" but rather
the degree of interdependence in a power structure. As if to
highlight this last conclusion, Jaques (35, pp. 265–66) noted:

> It is precisely because power relations may shift, while authority
> structure remains unchanged, that the firm's unanimity principle is
> of such value, for it allows the continuous testing out and explora-
> tion of the power situation by means of constructive discussion,
> instead of the intermittent testing of power which accompanies
> executive policies and actions which have not been agreed and
> which when unacceptable lead to a piling up of stress and to ex-
> plosive outcomes. Not that the unanimity principle solves questions
> of power relationships, rather it is to be seen as a mechanism for
> facilitating more constructive relationships and ensuring more real-
> istic compromises when the necessary motivations and skills exist in
> those concerned.

Jaques is suggesting that bringing coherence to the firm's power
structure may be facilitated by discussions, agreements, and
log-rolling among those whose power is affected and that this
may proceed more effectively if the group operates under a rule
of unanimity in reaching agreements. The role of unanimity is
to insure attachment to the decision finally reached and presumably also to those making it.

When the assignment of functions is equivocal or where it
is episodic, sometimes made and sometimes withdrawn, then
the individual is likely to react with disengagement from the
organization. Chowdhry and Pal (15), studying two Indian
cotton mills substantially similar in technology and organizational structure, noted that the managing agent of one who
failed to make fixed delegations of power (he went around
managers to their subordinates, for example) had a very high
turnover rate among his managerial staff and wide expressions
of dissatisfaction among those currently in management positions. The managing agent who made fixed assignments of

functions and then permitted the functionaries to fulfill them had relatively high morale among the members of his plant management. The old saw that "appropriate authority should be delegated with each responsibility" turns out to be an accurate description of efficient allocation of power in an organization, especially if we add that such delegations should be unequivocal and relatively inviolable.

A very common circumstance of business operations, where the assignment of function may be withdrawn or shifted under pressure, is illustrated by Ulrich, Booz, and Lawrence (58, p. 43) when they reported that the complaints about unfilled orders by the sales manager led the general manager to demand production at double what the foremen believed they could produce. This, in effect, says that the function of estimating effective productive capacity was taken away from foremen and performed at least temporarily by another member of management who was trying to placate a department and did not know the significant production facts as a ground for his own decision. It is not difficult to guess what the reaction of foremen was under such circumstance of a sudden and irrational redistribution of their power over estimating productive capacity.

One of the most universal reactions to an unstable distribution of functions among the ranks of management is intensive competition to gain control of desirable functions. Referring back to Jaques' study (35, p. 281), his observations led him to the conclusion that among the superintendents (foremen) rivalry was particularly noticeable when they individually and as a group held no defined position in the executive structure. This was made especially noticeable because the ongoing research was also designed to provide feedback to the organization and resulted in changes in ways of managing that made uncertain the functions of foremen in several periods of time.

The concept "power" has fascinated and eluded scholars for many centuries. We have only recently begun to make empirical studies of power and power relations that serve to illuminate the concept and demonstrate its significance for organizational analysis.

AUTHORITY

We are here using the concept of authority in the now classical sense described by Simon as the act of directing the actions of others in which they set aside their own basis of judgment in selecting the behavioral alternative. Certain limited but interesting features of the behavior of authority holders and the reactions of their subordinates to it will be examined here.

The most general view that authority holders in American industry take toward their subordinates seems to be that cooperation must be initiated and sustained by the authority holder. This belief of managers is well illustrated in the study of railroad track workers by Katz *et al.* (39, pp. 12–13), where it was found that 32 out of 72 of the foremen questioned said that the "men need watching" or that supervision was necessary to "get more work done." Brown, the top executive of the company studied by Jaques, concluded (11, p. 47) that all relations with subordinates involved at least advising and instructing —that no such thing as a pure "bottoms-up" management style is possible.

If we ask, "What areas of working behavior have built-in features that tend to support the authority relationship?" the general answer seems to be the technology of work. Thus Jaques (35, p. 262) concluded from his many observations over the three-year period of his study that in the English factory, "instructions accepted as necessitated by technological requirements carry greater authority than those which are not." On the other hand, Argyris (2, p. 114) found that, of all places, a bank trust department exhibited clearly an inversion of authority based on technological specialization. While the trust department employees clearly were given specific directions by the trust officers, there were situations in which the subordinates' technical knowledge exceeded that of their boss, and in such situations the subordinate actually wielded authority over the boss.

When the organization's formal structure does not specify the existence of an authority relationship, but one actually does exist, then the discourse between superior and subordinate seems to be materially modified. Jasinski (37, pp. 132–33), in the Yale study of the automobile assembly plant foremen, showed that there was a significant amount of contact between foremen and workers in the crews of other foremen. Under these circumstances the foremen "advised and made suggestions to rather than directed these non-subordinate operators. The relationship was marked by a considerable amount of non-job-related social exchange and joking." Furthermore, the direction of initiation of interaction was modified because the foreman's purely social contacts with outside subordinates were initiated 27 per cent of the time by them, while his own subordinates initiated social contacts (as distinct from work-related ones) with him only one half of 1 per cent of the time. On the other hand, to substitute non-job-related social exchange and joking in a formally specified authority relationship may, in fact, destroy part of the authority, as Jaques (35, p. 230) pointed out when one member of management actually told the managing director that the company executives were disturbed by the personal comments of the "big boss" because it was impossible completely to dissociate him from his role as the chief executive.

For those to whom the assumption of authority is a curse because it involves "pushing other people around," considerable comfort may be taken from the findings of Burns (12, p. 95), who studied four departmental managers. He matched the records of interactions between the department manager and his three managerial subordinates on 237 episodes. Of these, the boss reported that he gave instructions or decisions to his subordinates 165 times. Yet these three subordinates reported receiving instructions or decisions from the boss only 84 times. "Half the time, what the manager thought he was giving as in-

structions or decisions was being treated [by his subordi-
nates] as information or advice."

There seems to be a magic in communication acts. Orders,
from the originator's standpoint, become information or advice
when received by a subordinate. Is this the organizational
alchemist's dream come true—transmuting the base stuff of
orders, by the magic of merely passing them through authority
channels, into the gold of information and advice?

For those who find the authoritative role onerous, Jaques
(35, pp. 279–80) described four means he observed for avoiding authority, each with its own problems. The most obvious
shift in authoritative behavior was to change from direction giving to a consultative relationship. If Burns's finding is general,
then an actual shift to a very low level of order giving may
leave subordinates with the impression that orders are never
given. I think this is a wholly unrealistic situation ("group dynamics" to the contrary notwithstanding), which has greater
costs in the attenuation of the authority structure than the
gains made through subordinate participation and contribution.[10]

As the Glacier company moved increasingly toward consultative management and this involved downward distribution of
authority, as Jaques reported, one of the problems generated
was the tendency to by-pass levels of management in seeking
counsel downward or in offering information and suggestion
upward. Thus, in a sense, to make consultative management
work required that the consultation follow the chain of command. If it did not, then rivalries and conflicts arose from those
men in the chain of command who were by-passed.

A very significant feature of the Glacier company experiment
was the amount of self-analysis among executives as they went

---

[10] Indeed, if I may depart from the factual base of this chapter, it seems to
me that subordinate contribution and ingenuity are largely expended in the
realm of "nonformal" behavior, where subordinates make the boss's decisions
"look good" or make them work. It is doing the right and effective thing,
rather than what is literally ordered, that distinguishes the loyal, ingenious,
contributory subordinate.

about changing company managerial practices. Jaques pointed
out that this constant self-consciousness about authority acts,
even while they were being carried out, tended to demean the
situation of action and the actions taken.[11]

Finally, Jaques pointed to "mock democracy" as a coarse
way to deny the existence of authority without setting it aside.
One of the company executives attempted to assert, and
make stick, his contention that "I'm just an ordinary member
of this committee," when he was, in fact, the boss of all members of the committee. The subordinates rejected this "just a
common man" approach, and the committee did not function
effectively until the boss reassumed his chairmanship of it.

These apparently unco-ordinated aspects of the behavior of
authority holders and their subordinates' reactions to the exercise of authority all have one feature in common. They bring
into serious question whether effective administration can ever
be grounded in anything but a well-articulated and predic-
tively operating authority structure. We obviously distinguish
between "being authorative" and "being authoritarian." I wonder how many of the fervent advocates of "consultative management" (in all its many forms) make this same distinction?

CONTROL

In general, the expected or planned-for outcomes of organizational behavior have to be policed to insure some correspond-
ence between performance and plan. It is in this sense that we
shall examine formal controls of behavior in organizations. At
the end of this section we shall consider some consequences of
controls for other than the adaptive behavior of those respond-
ing to them, namely, evasive action.

In a pioneering study Argyris (4) examined the impact of
budget controls on those being controlled. He gave repeated

---

[11] I remember once as a visitor to the Harvard Graduate School of Business
being invited to sit in on a staff meeting of the faculty handling the famous
"Administrative Practices" course. It was here that I learned of the verb "To
ad pract," which meant to analyze the analysis. I had the impression that one
could end up an episode of "ad practing" with the feeling of lack of substance
and importance about the subject under consideration.

examples of short-run compliance with control standards that had either short- or long-run cost consequences for the organization. He reported instances of people who worked under fixed quotas of output, with some opportunity to select items to be worked on, choosing easy, rapidly completed jobs as fillers toward the end of the period in order to meet a quota (cf. the case of "Specialists Consultants, Inc.," in Dubin [26]). Blau (10) reported the same behavior among law-enforcement case analysts, who worked with an established case load of eight per month and who picked easy, fast cases toward the end of each month if they anticipated falling short of their quotas. Jasinski (38) reported a similar adaptation by foremen of "bleeding the line" in line production by sucking all work in progress through the measuring point (using augmented crews), in order to meet a production quota, but losing efficiency in the succeeding period until the line was refilled with work in progress.

An even more seriously distorting adaptive response to controls is reported by Blau (10), who pointed out that government employment-service interviewers were appraised by the number of interviews completed, resulting in their maximizing the number of interviews and not spending adequate time in finding jobs for clients (the obvious purpose of the interviews in the first place). This is a translation of means into ends, an apparently common response to output controls.

Perhaps the potentially most costly adaptation to controls is their deliberate evasion (on the assumption that the purposes of the controls were initially praiseworthy). Jasinski (38) reported instances of "making out with the pencil" as a means for giving the paper appearance of meeting expected standards, without actually doing so. Dalton (22) reported a comparable instance of evasion where local plant officials, through blandishments of, and subsequent conspiracy with, the central-office representative were able to evade cost-control checks imposed by the central office.

Remember we are here, in each instance, citing data dealing with *managerial* adaptation to controls and not that of rank-and-file workers. The phenomena of "banking" work to smooth out dips in individual output, of restriction of output, of "making with the pencil," and of outright cheating (a system-control firm recently advertised in the *Wall Street Journal* that employee fraud perpetrated on American business firms in 1961 was estimated to reach 1.5 billion dollars) have been too well documented at the worker level to need further elaboration here. What may be less comfortable for business executives to face openly is the reality that adaptive and evasive behavior is also characteristic of managers and executives.[12]

That the phenomenon of managerial adaptation to controls is not culture-bound is revealed by Granick (32), who pointed out that high rewards and glory attended the Soviet plant manager who set a new production record, so that there was pressure to do this at the expense of operating repairs and protective maintenance. This resulted in lower output in the subsequent period while the delayed maintenance was undertaken, but the manager had received his payoff for the overquota output of the earlier period. Berliner (9) noted the phenomenon of "storming" production toward the end of a quota period in Soviet industry to meet output standards, again at the expense of maintenance and also balanced output. Apparently, the adaptation of management men to the controls imposed on their output is independent of the larger social value systems in which they live. Indeed, one could even argue further that the nature of productive systems, requiring some predictability of output, will generate controls over output that are universal in their effects, regardless of the social system in which they are used. The gulf between values held and actual behavior is rather ironically revealed in Berliner's quote of Bulganin, who boasted that heads rolled each year in the management of the Soviet coal industry because managers did not meet quotas (a hard-boiled efficiency outlook for a top political

---

[12] This is highlighted by the recent price-fixing conspiracy practices among the giant electrical-goods firms when top managers asserted their "clean hands" by contending that subordinates' lawbreaking was hidden from their knowledge. This is an open admission, if true, that the controls on legal pricing policies were so inadequate in all the companies that lower executives could knowingly violate the law without fear of detection by their superiors.

leader in a welfare state), whereas it is less certain that American executives respond so sternly to the failures to meet quotas by their own subordinates (a remarkably welfare state-ish outlook for production-minded executives who proclaim their idolatry of efficiency). In any event, it seems highly probable that the severity of penalties incurred for failure to meet control standards will generate a proportional adaptive effort to make a face showing of compliance, regardless of the other costs involved to the organization.

The fear of criticism by bosses seems to be a central feature of managerial response to controls on their behavior. Jaques' long-term study of the managers of an English factory revealed that one of the strongest conventions among the divisional managers was never to criticize each other in front of their mutual boss (35, p. 281) but that criticism was not thereby suppressed, since it moved upward by skipping levels of management as it moved (35, p. 134). Furthermore, he found that the service and advisory specialists reported to the top executive criticisms of operating managers when they demanded wrong services or rejected offered advice. Dalton (21) has reported similar behavior by line executives that tended to impeach the competence of staff specialists through critical appraisal of them to top management.

Apparently the lines of functional specialization to be found in a firm provide natural but "hidden" channels of criticism flowing to top management, which encourage "ratting" on other functional specialists or at least deriding their performances to top executives.

We really do not have any published evidence that a secondary adaptation among managers to criticizing, or being criticized, is coalition and mutual protection against any effective criticism reaching top management through nonformal channels. We do have some reports (Ulrich, Booz, and Lawrence [58, p. 17], and Dalton [21], among others) that have pointed out that members of management tend to withhold information that would be useful to their superiors. This might conceivably be indirect evidence of "deals" that monitor the flow of adverse information upward. The only study that reveals the nature of these deals is one of Navy disbursing officers, made by Turner (57). He pointed out that there were services and/or goods in scarce supply and needed, resulting in reciprocal trades of goods and services that paid off about equally in both directions over a period of time. Presumably, very important trading chits in such reciprocity could be critical reports that it would be considered desirable to withhold from top management.

There is one more aspect of control that we shall consider—dealing with a technical feature of communication and order giving. The field of communications research has produced the analysis of messages and message units. Out of this have come some important findings about what the sociologist calls "definition of the situation." For example, Frick and Sumby (31), in studying the ability of military pilot trainees to complete control-tower messages, given initial clues, demonstrated that the estimated redundancy of such messages was approximately 96 per cent. They attribute most of the redundancy of the message units to the fact that each pilot perceived the situational context of the message, including the appropriate pilot procedural responses, so that each respondent was able to "define the situation" and predict the message content with very small cues. Such studies tell us a good deal inferentially about the possible unspoken and unmentioned aspects of orders, directives, and control standards. For those who are habituated to a situation and who share all significant participants' "definition of the situation," it takes little in the way of cueing to "get the message." It is the very habituation to the situational context that makes for high redundancy in communication and therefore leads to maximum communication with minimum interaction. In the context of control, minimum effort can be invested in control activities and in adaptations to them, because of the efficiency that a common definition of the situation gives to controlling methods.

It is remarkable to note that among managers and executives —the personnel of organizations whose position demands commitment to organization goals—there exists a strong tendency to meet formal criteria of performance, even if, in so doing, high but hidden costs are generated. It may be pertinent to suggest that specialists in control systems, engineers and accountants particularly, might find additional sources of efficiency in eliminating some of the costs of managerial adaptation to controls that evade their spirit but conform to their letter.

LEADERSHIP

Most of what has been examined up to this point has dealt with some aspect of leadership. There remain, however, some specialized facets of organizational leadership to which we now turn. It should be understood that this is not intended to be a full-scale coverage.

There is an important distinction that needs to be made between (A) the atmosphere of a group that may be attributable to the behaviors of its leader and (B) the structure of the group and the ways in which leadership behavior both determines and sustains it. Most of the literature on leadership styles, of which Argyris' study of a single executive in action is an excellent example (1), deals with the atmosphere created by a leader's actions and especially with the atmospheres generated by "authoritarian" behavior as distinct from authoritative behavior. In the attempt to exorcise authoritarianism from managerial practice, the group-structure facet of the problem has been largely neglected. Let us turn to it.

Jaques (35, p. 243) came to the sweeping conclusion that "as the General Manager assumed more fully his leadership mantle, his subordinates in turn accepted theirs." This conclusion really stemmed from the natural experiments in managing that were introduced in the Glacier company, on the advice of Jaques, acting as consultant. Thus he was able to observe a variety of leadership roles that were played by the general manager and to contrast subordinate responses to each of these variations. Jaques' conclusion tells us, first of all, that there is a distinctive role of leadership in groups (confirmed many times over in the study of all kinds of groups) and that members expect this role to be fulfilled. Furthermore, he is asserting that until this role is filled adequately, the other members of the group are disorganized in terms of being able to define *their* roles. We see this more concretely in the study by Chowdhry and Pal (15) in the contrast between the two managing agents of two Indian cotton mills, one of whom violated the chain of command and produced disorganization in the ranks of his managerial subordinates. This managing agent, by his actions, never permitted the structure of the managing group to settle down and actually threatened the standing and position of each subordinate in the group structure. He had high turnover, low morale, and all the other symptoms of discontent among his managers as a result.

We can see this same influence of leader behavior in structuring the group in another dimension. Weiss (59, p. 32) pointed out that a leader should not assign work to anyone who lacks the legitimate characteristics to perform the tasks. Although he analyzed a research group in which the issue of legitimacy was highly visible, the conclusion has general relevance. For example, to assign an accounting task to the executive in charge of engineering may rupture the relations between the assigning executive, the chief engineer, and the chief accountant, because at least the last executive would consider the engineer lacking in legitimacy to handle the problem (quite aside from the question of technical competence). Thus a leader may have very significant effects on his subordinate managerial team if he fails to observe the legitimacy to perform in those to whom task assignments are made.

A leader, then, has to discriminate between the legitimacy and nonlegitimacy of those to whom task assignments are made. He also has to recognize clearly the structure of authority in the managerial team and act to preserve it. The question then arises as to whether there are measurable characteristics of leaders that indicate an ability to make such discriminations. As part of a long-term research project, Cleven and Fiedler (16) used an instrument measuring the ability to distinguish characteristics of most- and least-liked working associates with steel-mill open-hearth crew supervisors. The "heat" record was used as the criterion of supervisory competence. The study showed that pit foremen and melters—the supervisors most directly involved in open-hearth operations—discriminated much more sharply between most- and least-preferred co-workers if they had good production records than if their records were poor. This tells us that people with a direct command, who get good output from their subordinates, can also perceive distinctions among these subordinates.

If this is a general skill of good supervisors having a direct command, then we have here a logical closure. Good supervisors have to structure the group they lead. There seems to be evidence that such a skill exists, insofar as the ability to discriminate among people is a necessary condition to being able to assign them to an appropriate position in the group structure.

In further support of the leadership role of structuring the group, the study by Fleishman *et al.* (29, pp. 98–99), in spite of its focus on leadership "atmosphere," concluded that ". . . the foremen who were regarded by their supervisors as most proficient actually operated in the most structuring fashion"; and then added: "The more efficient foremen, as rated by the boss, are inclined to show more initiation structure and less consideration."

Perhaps enough has now been said to indicate that we must analytically disentangle the leadership function of creating and sustaining a group "atmosphere" from the function of creating and sustaining a group "structure." There are undoubtedly some interactions between these two facets of leadership. There must also be some independence between them. It is to this independence that we have given attention and toward which considerable further research must be directed.

A minor but important point about leadership behavior is that the leader may be a key person in symbolizing the organization charter, as Bakke (7) has pointed out, and that, in the process, subordinates can make organizational norms their own without explicit direction from the boss. Marcson (44, pp. 104–5), studying scientists in American industry, showed that research scientists themselves were self-selecting of projects in terms of their fit with company goals. The administrators of research and development departments did not have to tell their scientists directly that certain kinds of projects or studies in certain areas were more pertinent to company needs than others. This came to be understood by the working scientists, and they made their choices of projects accordingly. Here we have a supplement to the conclusion reached in considering authority, where it was pointed out that subordinates transmute orders into information. Subordinates also anticipate what is believed and expected and act out this expectation without direction. Again, some of the curse is taken off authoritativeness by the ability of subordinates to anticipate and act out what *would have been* an order or suggestion and thus obviate the need for ever giving it in the first place.

While the executive is in constant *contact with* the people of his working environment, as we have already discovered, there is strong evidence that he is *isolated from* this environment. Drucker (25, pp. 89–93), in his study of General Motors, made a very strong point of the isolation of the executives of that firm from the lower reaches of their own organization and also from the larger social environment in which the firm operated. Jaques (35, p. 278) showed that executive leaders were isolated from the led group within their own organization. This executive isolation breeds provincialism in outlook, giving rise to the kind of thinking, sincerely believed by its author no doubt, that "what's good for General Motors is good for the country." On the other hand, the isolation, even with provincialism, may be highly functional in the pursuit of innovation as a protection against the need to conform to going ways of thinking. Perhaps the career of Henry Ford is illustrative of this facet of executive isolation.

The executive's position has its costs, and they may be high at the personal level. Bakke (7, pp. 41–42) has pointed out that there was a high level of fatigue associated with being an executive, even in a telephone company, a public utility with no problems of competition. Coates and Pellegrin (17) reported career supervisors, men who had reached their ceiling of promotion, pointing to the strain on their bosses and even labeling it "industrial suicide." Giving concrete specification to one of these stresses, Jaques (35, pp. 223–24) indicated that the top executive filled a lightening-rod function for trouble. When managerial subordinates had problems, there was a strong inclination to route them through the managing director of this English company. This lightening-rod function for attracting trouble was perhaps best symbolized by the slogan that former President Truman kept on his desk: "The buck stops here."

We have pointed to some of the behaviors of leaders that provide insight about the functions of leadership in organizations. Obviously, much more needs to be studied before we achieve full understanding. It seems clear that a good share of such study should be focused on the actual behaviors of executives.

IN CONCLUSION

Let me repeat the admonition with which I started. I have tried to avoid attitudinal data and to concentrate on the behaviors of managers as they have been systematically observed. This has led to conclusions that are at variance with some of the more popular ones now filling the pages of the literature on administration.[13]

It is astonishing that our allegedly activist society—the society of doers ("the difficult we do immediately, the impossible

---

[13] A simple example of this will suffice. Pelz (48) concluded that workers' attachment to the supervisor was the product of their perception that the supervisor was influential in the organization. Likert (41), using Pelz's conclusion, then built a model of organizational behavior based on this as a central idea, in spite of the fact that the original measure of "supervisor influence" was contrived out of responses to questions asked for another purpose (and had a very low "face validity" in my humble opinion) and in spite of the fact that Mann and Hoffman (42), working in the same research institute and making specific test of Pelz's conclusion, came to contradictory results in studying power-plant employees. I admire and respect Likert's skill in model building and that of many of his contemporaries, who have high analytical abilities and first-class technical skills in research. Perhaps it would be productive of immediate and very substantial advances if good behavioral scientists rediscovered *behavior* as their central datum.

takes a little longer")—is one in which most of the public and academic thinking about management of enterprises rests on subjective data. We use attitude data both to discover and to justify management practices. We have relatively little data on the actual behaviors of managers. If this chapter has done nothing more than to alert the students of administration to turn to the study of behavior, unvarnished and uncluttered with subjective materials, it will have served its purpose. It is also hoped that this analysis of a sample of good behavioral studies of managers may point some directions in which organization theory will evolve.

REFERENCES

1. ARGYRIS, C. *Executive Leadership.* New York: Harper & Bros., 1953.
2. ————. *Organization of a Bank.* New Haven: Labor and Management Center, Yale University, 1954.
3. ————. *Personality and Organization.* New York: Harper & Bros., 1957.
4. ————. *The Impact of Budgets on People.* New York: Controllership Institute, 1952.
5. ————. "Understanding Human Behavior in Organizations: One Viewpoint," in M. HAIRE (ed.), *Modern Organization Theory,* chap. 5. New York: John Wiley & Sons, 1959.
6. BAKER, H., and FRANCE, R. R. *Centralization and Decentralization in Industrial Relations.* Princeton: Industrial Relations Section, Princeton University, 1954.
7. BAKKE, E. W. *Bonds of Organization.* New York: Harper & Bros., 1950.
8. BENDIX, R. "Bureaucratization in Industry," in A. KORNHAUSER *et al.* (eds.), *Industrial Conflict,* chap. 12. New York: McGraw-Hill Book Co., 1954.
9. BERLINER, J. "A Problem in Soviet Business Management," *Administrative Science Quarterly,* Vol. I (June, 1956), pp. 87–101.
10. BLAU, P. *Dynamics of Bureaucracy.* Chicago: University of Chicago Press, 1955.
11. BROWN, W. *Exploration in Management.* New York: John Wiley & Sons, 1960.
12. BURNS, T. "The Direction of Activity and Communication in a Departmental Executive Group," *Human Relations,* Vol. VII (1954), pp. 73–97.
13. CARLSON, S. *Executive Behaviour.* Stockholm: Stromborgs, 1951.

14. CHAMBERLAIN, N. *Management in Motion.* New Haven: Labor and Management Center, Yale University, 1950.

15. CHOWDHRY, K., and PAL, A. K. "Production Planning and Organizational Morale," *Human Organization,* Vol. XV (Winter, 1957), pp. 11–16.

16. CLEVEN, W. A., and FIEDLER, F. E. "Interpersonal Perceptions of Open-Hearth Foremen and Steel Production," *Journal of Applied Psychology,* Vol. XL (1956), pp. 312–14.

17. COATES, C. H., and PELLEGRIN, R. J. "Executives and Supervisors: Contrasting Self-Conceptions and Conceptions of Each Other," *American Sociological Review,* Vol. XXII (April, 1957), pp. 217–20.

18. CYERT, R. M., SIMON, H. A., and TROW, D. B. "Observation of a Business Decision," *Journal of Business,* XXIX (October, 1956), pp. 237–48.

19. CYERT, R. M., DILL, W. R., and MARCH, J. G. "The Role of Expectations in Business Decision Making," *Administrative Science Quarterly,* Vol. III (December, 1958), pp. 307–40.

20. DALE, E. R. *Planning and Developing the Company Organization Structure.* New York: American Management Association, 1952.

21. DALTON, M. "Conflicts between Staff and Line Managerial Officers," *American Sociological Review,* Vol. XV (June, 1950), pp. 342–51.

22. ———. "Managing the Managers," *Human Organization,* Vol. XIV (Fall, 1955), pp. 4–10.

23. ———. *Men Who Manage.* New York: John Wiley & Sons, 1959.

24. DILL, W. R. "Environment as an Influence on Managerial Autonomy," *Administrative Science Quarterly,* Vol. II (March, 1958), pp. 409–43.

25. DRUCKER, P. F. *The Concept of the Corporation.* New York: John Day, 1946.

26. DUBIN, R. *Human Relations in Administration.* 2d ed. Englewood Cliffs, N.J.: Prentice-Hall, Inc., 1961.

27. ———. "Industrial Workers' Worlds: A Study of 'Central Life Interests' of Industrial Workers," *Social Problems,* Vol. III (January, 1956), pp. 131–42.

28. ———. *The World of Work.* Englewood Cliffs, N.J.: Prentice-Hall, Inc., 1958.

29. FLEISHMAN, E. A., HARRIS, E. F., and BURTT, H. E. *Leadership and Supervision in Industry.* Columbus: Ohio State University Press, 1955.

30. FOX, W. M. "Group Reaction to Two Types of Conference Leadership," *Human Relations,* Vol. X (1957), pp. 279–89.

31. FRICK, F. C., and SUMBY, W. H. "Control Tower Language," *Journal of the Acoustical Society of America,* Vol. XXIV (November, 1952), pp. 595–96.

32. GRANICK, D. *Management of the Industrial Firm in the U.S.S.R.* New York: Columbia University Press, 1954.

33. GUEST, R. H. "Of Time and the Foreman," *Personnel*, May, 1956.

34. HAIRE, M. "Biological Models and Empirical Histories of the Growth of Organizations," in M. HAIRE (ed.), *Modern Organization Theory*, chap. 10. New York: John Wiley & Sons, 1959.

35. JAQUES, ELLIOTT. *The Changing Culture of a Factory.* New York: Dryden Press, 1952.

36. JANOWITZ, M. R., and DELANEY, W. "The Bureaucrat and the Public: A Study of Informational Perspectives," *Administrative Science Quarterly*, Vol. II (September, 1957), pp. 141–62.

37. JASINSKI, F. J. "Foreman Relations Outside the Work Group," *Personnel*, Vol. XXXIII (September, 1956), pp. 130–36.

38. ——. "Use and Misuse of Efficiency Controls," *Harvard Business Review*, Vol. XXXIV (July–August, 1956), pp. 105–12.

39. KATZ, D., et al. *Productivity, Supervision, and Morale among Railroad Workers.* Ann Arbor: Survey Research Center, University of Michigan, 1951.

40. KOONTZ, H., and O'DONNELL, C. *Principles of Management.* 2d ed. New York: McGraw-Hill Book Co., 1959.

41. LIKERT, R. "A Motivation Approach to a Modified Theory of Organization and Management," in M. HAIRE (ed.), *Modern Organization Theory*, chap. 7. New York: John Wiley & Sons, 1959.

42. MANN, F. C., and HOFFMAN, L. R. *Automation and the Worker.* New York: Henry Holt & Co., 1960.

43. MARCH, J. G., and SIMON, H. A. *Organizations.* New York: John Wiley & Sons, 1958.

44. MARCSON, S. *The Scientist in American Industry.* Princeton: Industrial Relations Section, Princeton University, 1960.

45. MCMURRY, R. N. "Recruitment, Dependency, and Morale in the Banking Industry," *Administrative Science Quarterly*, Vol. III (June, 1958), pp. 87–106.

46. MELMAN, S. *Decision Making and Productivity.* Oxford: Basil Blackwell, 1958.

47. PELZ, D. C. "Interaction and Attitudes between Scientists and Auxiliary Staff," *Administrative Science Quarterly*, Vol. IV (December, 1959), pp. 321–36.

48. ——. "Leadership within a Hierarchical Organization," *Journal of Social Issues*, Vol. VII (1951), pp. 49–55.

49. PIERSOL, D. T. "Communication Practices of Supervisors in a Mid-Western Corporation," *Advanced Management*, Vol. XXIII (February, 1958), pp. 20–21.

50. PONDER, Q. D. "The Effective Manufacturing Foreman," *Proceedings of the Tenth Annual Meeting, Industrial Relations Research Association*, pp. 41–54. Madison, Wis.: The Association, 1958.

51. RICHARDSON, F. L. W., and WALKER, C. R. *Human Relations in an Expanding Company.* New Haven: Labor and Management Center, Yale University, 1948.

52. ROETHLISBERGER, F. J. "The Foreman: Master and Victim of Double Talk," *Harvard Business Review,* Vol. XXIII (Spring, 1945), pp. 285–94.

53. SAYLES, L. R. *Behavior of Industrial Work Groups.* New York: John Wiley & Sons, 1958.

54. SAYLES, L. R., and CHAPPLE, E. D. *The Measure of Management.* New York: Macmillan Co., 1961.

55. SIMPSON, R. L. "Vertical and Horizontal Communication in Formal Organization," *Administrative Science Quarterly,* Vol. IV (September, 1959), pp. 188–96.

56. STOGDILL, R. M., and SHARTLE, C. L. *Methods in the Study of Administrative Leadership.* Columbus: Bureau of Business Research, Ohio State University, 1955.

57. TURNER, R. "The Navy Disbursing Officer as a Bureaucrat," *American Sociological Review,* Vol. XII (June, 1947), pp. 342–48.

58. ULRICH, D. N., BOOZ, D. R., and LAWRENCE, P. R. *Management Behavior and Foreman Attitude: A Case Study.* Cambridge: Harvard Graduate School of Business Administration, 1950.

59. WEISS, R. S. *Processes of Organization.* Ann Arbor: Survey Research Center, University of Michigan, 1956.

60. WHYTE, W. F. *Human Relations in the Restaurant Industry.* New York: McGraw-Hill Book Co., 1948.

61. ZINCK, C. "The Foreman and Productivity," *Advanced Management,* Vol. XXIII (January, 1958), pp. 12–16.

2

THE INTEGRATION OF THE INDIVIDUAL AND THE ORGANIZATION

Chris Argyris[1]

THIS paper has two objectives. The first is to present (hopefully) some relatively new concepts in organizational leadership and structure. The second objective stems partially from the fact that the suggestions regarding leadership and structure imply that individual and organizational development ought to be valued. Although as a researcher I have no interest in persuading anyone to accept these values, I do feel an obligation to those who may wish to value these values (and I do), to embed them in as solid a theoretical and empirical foundation as possible. Concerning the theoretical foundation, I shall attempt to embed my suggestions in the construct of organization. I do so for two reasons. First, I believe that organization is a basic phenomenon of existence. It can be found everywhere and on many different levels of analysis (e.g., individual, group, societal, etc.). This leads me to the second reason. I have a value of striving to make some contribution to the objective of "unity of knowledge" where several disciplines on

---
[1] This research has been undertaken with the financial support of a National Institute of Mental Health grant, 3M-9128. This excellent financial support is gratefully acknowledged.

The paper was presented at the University of Wisconsin, School of Commerce, May, 1961.

different levels of analysis are systematically related into a meaningful whole.[2] I believe that the construct of organization is a valid path toward this objective. As to the empirical work, I have just begun to conduct field research to test the validity of the suggestions. Consequently, I have few data to report at this time.

One final word by way of introduction. Parts of the paper deal with values in a descriptive manner. Other parts deal with the same values normatively. It is important that we keep these two issues separated but at the same time show how they are related to each other. In an attempt to do so, I use a relatively new field of philosophy called "axiology," with which one can attempt to relate the theoretical construct of organization to the "axiologically good" organization. Once the "axiologically good" organization is understood, I then use it to construct a bridge for the normative issues implied in my suggestions regarding organizational leadership and structure. It is important to emphasize that the "axiologically good" organization is an analytic and systematic device and is not a normative concept.

SOME REASONS FOR INTEGRATING THE INDIVIDUAL AND THE ORGANIZATION

In *Personality and Organization* I suggest that the formal organization and the administrative control system typically used in complex organizations may be viewed as parts of a grand strategy to organize human effort to achieve specific objectives or intended consequences; that this strategy is based on such "principles" of administration as specialization of work, chain of command, unity of direction, and span of control; that the strategy creates a complex of organizational imperatives that tend to require individuals to experience dependence and submissiveness and to utilize few of their relatively peripheral abilities; that the degree of dependency, submissiveness, etc., required by the organization tends to increase as one goes

---

[2] Chris Argyris, *Understanding Organizational Behavior* (Homewood, Ill.: Dorsey Press, Inc., 1961), chap. i.

down the chain of command and as the job requirements and managerial controls direct the individual; that they decrease as one goes up the chain of command and as the individual is able to control the job requirements.

Those individuals who aspire toward being independent, creative, etc., may adapt to this impoverished work world by such activities as absenteeism, turnover, trade union, apathy, indifference, gold bricking, rate setting, increasing emphasis on material rewards and decreasing emphasis on human or psychosocial rewards, and by reversing their own self-actualizing process and becoming more directed toward dependence, subordination, and alienation.

Typically, administrators view these "informal activities" as "outputs" of "irresponsible" people rather than as unintended consequences of the very strategy that they use to organize and control human effort. Consequently, they typically take corrective action by tightening the old and creating new managerial controls and leadership patterns that ironically tend to increase the dependency, submissiveness, etc., that the employees experience. This causes the employees to increase their informal activities, which, in turn, causes administrators to increase the use of controls, and so we have a series of feedback mechanisms that will act to increase the difficulties.

One further word: The generalizations above, I suggest, are valid for *any* formal organization (in our culture) based on formal "scientific" management principles. Thus they are meant to be valid for schools, hospitals, government agencies, unions, Scout troops, churches, etc. Most of the illustrations in this paper will deal with industrial settings simply because it is in this area that I conduct most of my research.

One way of looking at the implications of this point of view is that both the organization and the individual will suffer. The individuals may become apathetic and indifferent or so hostile, aggressive, and, in either case, so alienated that their mental health can be seriously effected.[3] The organization in

---

[3] Chris Argyris, "Individual Actualization in Complex Organizations," *Mental Hygiene*, Vol. XLIV, No. 2 (April, 1960), pp. 226–37.

turn may eventually become so rigid and inefficient that it will deteriorate.

Is there anything that can be done to create organizations that will provide a better "fit" for the individual, thereby hopefully enhancing the organization's and the individual's probabilities for survival and growth? Is there anything the individual can do to become a more fully functioning, committed human being where he can give of himself without giving *up* himself, thereby enhancing his mental health and the organization's probability for survival and growth?

During the past several years I have been trying to do some thinking about these questions. The objective has been to develop some testable hypothesis that can serve as the beginning for a long-range research project. As you shall see in a moment, the going has been tough and the progress seems—especially looking back—quite small.

THE VALUES IMPLICIT IN THIS RESEARCH

The questions that I raise about the individual and the organization imply that I value individual and organizational health and development. Indeed I do. I also believe that they are so intimately interrelated that one cannot have optimum amounts of one without optimum amounts of the other.

This belief implies that the integration of the individual needs and organizational demands not only is possible but is necessary if each is to survive and develop. How can these two organisms, developed by the use of two seemingly different strategies, be integrated?

Formal organization and the individual are basically organisms or organizations at different levels of analysis. There is extensive thinking and literature to suggest that organizations have some basic properties that are common to all levels of analysis. If organizations have properties that are common to all levels of analysis, then this might be a point at which to begin.

After an extensive examination of much of the relevant literature in the physical, biological, and social science, I concluded that all human or social organizations at any level of analysis may be said to have the following essential properties: An organization is:

1. A plurality of parts
2. Maintaining themselves through their interrelatedness, and
3. Achieving specific objective(s)
4. While accomplishing 2 and 3, adapting to the external environment, thereby
5. Maintaining their interrelated state of the parts

SOME CLARIFYING COMMENTS RELATED TO THE DEFINITION OF ESSENTIAL PROPERTIES OF ORGANIZATION

1. What is a part? Since the properties above are considered essential to any living organism, one cannot define a priori what is the nature of the "part." In any given empirical case, however, the "part" can be defined to mean individuals, small groups, departments, etc. The important point being made is that an organism must have more than one part (no matter what the size of the part).

2. Moreover, from the statement "maintaining themselves through their interrelatedness" we hypothesize that a part must be an organic part. An organic part is one that performs some function(s) without which the whole cannot exist and, without the whole, the part cannot survive. This implies that there is a state of mutual dependence among the parts and between the parts and the whole.[4]

The exact degree of mutual dependence cannot be ascertained without reference to a particular organization and therefore requires empirical research. If one examines the experimental literature, one finds an interesting trend away from the notion of "master" parts or "governing" parts. For example, it used to be said that the heart and the brain are "master" parts. Yet a more "minor" part, such as the excretory system, if disabled long enough, can cause death. It seems that, as long as one is dealing with living, open systems, whatever part one

---

[4] L. K. Frank, "Genetic Psychology and Its Prospects," *American Journal of Orthopsychiatry*, Vol. XXI, No. 2 (July, 1951), No. 3, pp. 506–22.

judges essential is largely a function of what one wants to consider essential in his research design. Our notions of dominant parts, therefore, tend to evolve from the way we have been studying organization and not necessarily from the nature of living organizations per se. If one conducts an experiment by varying some variable systematically, then obviously it will be dominant. It is when the other variables are really permitted to exist in their "natural state" that "dominance" turns out to be more difficult to ascertain. Therefore, in living organisms, as research increases, the dominance of parts is being replaced with the idea of *essentiality* of parts. Under the new concept, no one part is seen as being necessarily more important than others.

L. K. Frank summarizes the position as follows:

> When we look more intently at man's internal environment, we find a number of organ systems, each performing its specialized functions in the internal environment which is highly organized and interrelated. This internal organization, like the organization we are discovering in the rest of nature, is not a relation of dominance and submission, of a governing or dictator organ exercising control over all others, as we have long been accustomed to think. The kind of organization we find is a patterned activity in which all the specialized organ systems and functional processes constitute the organization and maintain the organized whole by the way each articulates, synchronizes, compensates, and otherwise operates in relation to all the others. The organization arises and is maintained, therefore, by the specialized constituent parts which thereby create the organized whole and this organized whole in turn, reacts back upon the parts to keep them articulated and synchronized. This is the same kind of organization or field found in the atom, the molecule, the crystal and other orderly configurations and also in human society.[5]

3. As we have seen above, all parts are organized so that a particular objective or objectives can be achieved. Thus the third essential property of the systems being considered is that they must have conscious or unconscious objective(s).

4. All organizations are assumed to be embedded in an en-

---

[5] Lawrence K. Frank, *Nature and Human Nature: Man's New Image of Himself* (New Brunswick, N.J.: Rutgers University Press, 1951), pp. 53–54.

vironment that is continually changing and thus continually influencing the organization. A major task of any organism is to adapt to its environment either by changing its own internal arrangement and objectives or by striving to change the environment.

Exactly where the organization ends and the environment begins is a difficult question and one that has consumed many hours of philosophical and empirical analysis. For our purposes we shall simply say that it is our task to isolate any system from its environment by trying to determine, as Smith[6] and Levy[7] suggest, "how little" of the environment need be included in our description in order to render the behavior of the system neutral to, or independent of, the rest of the environment, i.e., to determine whether the whole can be understood in terms of its parts.

Organizations are therefore "open systems" continually influenced by and influencing their environment. Consequently, one cannot predict completely the future of an organization by knowing only its present state.[8] Another characteristic of an open system is that the output[9] does not necessarily vary systematically with any known input.[10] Thus, if input is increased or decreased, the output may not necessarily vary systematically with the input changes. Nor is there a constant relationship between output and input.

5. The essential characteristics of any living organization are hypothesized to be (1) achieving its objectives, (2) maintain-

---

[6] Homer W. Smith, "Organism and Environment: Dynamic Oppositions," *Adaptation*, pp. 26–27.

[7] Hyman Levy, *The Universe of Science* (New York: Appleton-Century, 1933).

[8] Ludwig von Bertallanfey, "Problems of General System Theory," *Human Biology*, Vol. XXIII, No. 4 (December, 1951), pp. 302–12.

[9] Output is the desired product of the system plus other relevant consequences of functioning.

[10] Input is anything put into the system that affects the output. See John D. Trimmer, *Response of Physical Systems* (New York: John Wiley & Sons, 1950), chap. 1. These definitions are stated by John B. Knox, "Productivity and Human Relations: Some Basic Principles," *Proceedings of the 16th Congress of the International Institute of Sociology, Beaune, France, September 19–26, 1954.*

ing itself internally, and (3) adapting to the external environment. These three sets of complex activities are called the *organizational core activities.*

The reader may wonder how organizational growth is to be treated. It is at this point that we must differentiate between living social and biological organisms. Growth is inherent in the biological organism. Growth is not seen as inherent in social organizations. There does not seem to be anything "in" a social organization that is comparable with the role of the genes in biological organisms that guarantees a certain degree of growth if the system is permitted to develop naturally.

This does not mean that growth of social organizations is to be ignored. On the contrary, growth is viewed as an important process, the nature of which is dependent on the socioeconomic environment in which the organization is embedded. The cause of growth in a social organization is hypothesized to be related to the effective achievement of any one or a combination of the core activities. In other words, if a social organization grows, it is related to (1) the achievement of the objective(s) and/or (2) the maintenance of the internal system and/or (3) the adaptation to the external environment.

AXIOLOGY AND ORGANIZATIONAL THEORY

These are the essential or intrinsic properties of human organizations. The next step leads us to the utilization of a relatively new field in philosophy called "axiology," or the science of values. Professor Robert Hartman describes the science of value as follows:

> The *science* of value is to value as the science of botany, for example, is to a rose: it does not smell; or as the symbols of Einstein are to the atomic bomb: they do not explode. There are no big blasts in a science, no excitement, no drama, except, perhaps, the excitement that comes from precise thinking and the drama that comes from intellectual discovery. The science of value is an intellectual, not a valuational, enterprise. The value analyst does not value but analyses value, just as the analyst of motion does not move but analyses motion.[11]

---

[11] Robert S. Hartman, "The Science of Value," in *New Knowledge in Human Values* (ed. A. H. Maslow) (New York: Harper & Bros., 1959), pp. 13–37.

Something is good axiologically, when it fulfills the definition of its concept.[12] An axiologically good organization, therefore, is one which fulfills or approximates the essential or intrinsic properties of its definition. A word of caution. As we shall see, there is a difference between the axiologically good and the normative good. It is the former that we are focusing on at this time. We shall get to the latter in a moment.

We may hypothesize that a good (still axiologically speaking) organization is one that fulfills or approximates these essential properties. If this is the case, then the first step would be to develop a model with which we can measure the degree that any given empirical organization (individual or social) fulfills or approximates the essential properties of organizations.

Our definition of organization contains several essential properties. Each of these properties implies a specific state of affairs. For example, the first property assumes that, instead of the whole being created or directed by the actions of one or a subset of parts, it is created through the interrelationships of all the parts.

In this way we are able to build a model of six interrelated dimensions. An organization approximates the axiologically good organization as its activities mirror the states of affairs at the right ends of these continua. An organization approximates the axiologically not-good organization as its activities mirror the states of affairs at the left ends of these continua.

THE AXIOLOGICALLY GOOD AND NOT-GOOD ORGANIZATION

The following dimension may be used to describe the axiologically good and not-good organization (see Table 1):

1. From a state of affairs wherein *a part (or a subset of parts) directs the organizational "core activities" (achieving the objectives, maintaining the internal system, and adapting*

[12] Robert S. Hartman, "General Theory of Value," *Philosophie: Chronique des Années 1949–1955* (New York: Institute of International Philosophy, UNESCO, 1958).

to the environment) to the state of affairs wherein these core activities are directed through the interrelationships of all the parts.

According to our concept of the properties of a living organization, the organization achieves its objectives, maintains itself internally, and adapts to its environment through the interrelationships of the parts. It follows that in any given empirical case the more any part (or subset of parts) controls these "core

TABLE 1

AXIOLOGICALLY GOOD AND NOT-GOOD ORGANIZATION

Not-Good Organization	Good Organization
I. One part (subset of parts) control the whole	The whole is created and controlled through interrelationships of all parts
II. Awareness of plurality of parts	Awareness of pattern of parts
III. Unable to influence its internally oriented core activities	Able to influence internally oriented core activities as it desires
IV. Unable to influence its externally oriented core activities.	Able to influence externally oriented core activities as it desires
V. Ineffective problem solving	Effective problem solving
VI. Nature of core activities influenced by the present	Nature of core activities influenced by the past, the present, and the future

activities," the less that given case approximates the good organization.

A dimension may be defined, therefore, whose one end represents a state of affairs wherein the objectives are achieved and the whole is maintained internally and adapts to its environment as a result of the activity of one or a subset of parts. The other end of this dimension would represent a state of affairs wherein these core activities were carried out through the interrelationship of all the parts.

This dimension assumes, as is pointed out above, that in a living organization each part has some influence or authority over the core activities. This does not necessarily mean that all parts have equal influence. It means that the amount of influence (or authority) among the parts is so distributed that, no matter where it is, the discreteness of that part plus its activities of feeding upon and feeding back to the other parts is not controlled by any other part or subset of parts. To put this another way, each part has that degree of influence that it requires to maintain itself and perform its function in the whole.

2. *From a state of awareness of the organization as a plurality of parts to a state of awareness of the organization as a pattern of parts.*

This dimension is necessary when we consider the special case of organizations that have human beings acting as their agents.[13] As Lewin and others point out, in order to have a lawful study of human behavior one must study such behavior from the perception of the individual whose behavior one is trying to understand. It is not enough, therefore, that the organization be a patterning of parts when human beings are the agents. It is important that the participants *perceive* the organization as an interrelated whole, objective-achieving, adapting organism, (i.e., as unity). The greater the number of participants who perceive the wholeness of the organization, the more their *behavior will create a system that approximates an axiologically good organization.* The more the participants acting as agents perceive it as a plurality of parts, achieving related or unrelated objectives, etc., the less the organization will approximate the "good" organization.

3. *From a state in which the organization[14] is unable to influence its internally oriented core activities (achieving the objectives, maintaining the internal system) to a state in which it can influence these activities as the organization desires.*

The third dimension is, I believe, a special case of the first two. Because of its importance in resolving problems, it is differentiated into a discrete dimension.

---

[13] For an excellent discussion of the role of "agents" see E. W. Bakke, *Bonds of Organization* (New York: Harper & Bros., 1950).

[14] May I again remind the reader that when I use the word "organization" in such a context I mean the individuals acting as agents for the organization.

If the organization is hypothesized to be a dynamic open system, continually achieving objectives, influencing and being influenced by its environment, then one may hypothesize that the organization not only should be able to direct itself and be aware of itself but should be able to modify any of its internal core activities as becomes necessary. The greater the freedom to modify these core activities, the closer any given organization approximates the "good" organization.

Implicit in this dimension is the assumption that in the axiologically good organization no activity should be beyond the control of the participants of the organization. No activity becomes compulsive, rigidified activity that continues independent of the external stimuli and/or the desires of the participants. Organizational activities that continue against the desires of, and are beyond the control of, the participants are compulsive activities. Such a state of affairs suggests that there may be something wrong. More of this later.

4. *From a state in which the organization is ineffective in problem solving to a state in which it is optimally effective in problem solving.*

In this dimension the focus is on the nature of the problem-solving processes that must exist if freedom and desire for change are to lead to effective changes.

One may hypothesize that the organization's problem-solving effectiveness will tend to increase as it (1) increases its awareness of the relevant stimuli influencing it at any time, (2) is able to explore the relevant actions, and (3) is able to carry out the action selected by the participants. To put this another way, it seems possible to hypothesize that effectiveness in problem solving increases as the organization (1) is able to recognize its problems, (2) searches and locates the relevant alternatives, (3) determines accurately the consequences that follow from each alternative, and (4) chooses the most satisfactory alternative (or set of alternatives).[15] The effectiveness of the problem solving may be hypothesized to *decrease* as it

---

[15] Herbert Simon, "Recent Advances in Organization Theory," *Research Frontiers in Politics and Government* (Washington: Brookings Institution, 1958), pp. 33–34.

(1) is not able to recognize its problems, (2) is unable to search and locate the relevant alternatives, (3) is unable to determine accurately the consequences that follow from each alternative, and (4) is unable to choose the most satisfactory (to it) alternative possible.

By utilizing dimensions 1, 2, and 3 in our model, we may also hypothesize that the diagnosis and the solution of the problem should include as many of the parts of the organization as relevant. The more any given organization's problem-solving processes takes into account dimensions 1, 2, and 3, the closer that given organization approximates the axiologically good organization.

5. *From a state in which the organization is unable to influence its externally oriented activities to a state in which it can influence these activities as the organization desires.*

The fifth dimension is similar to the fourth except that it is concerned with the organization's relationship to the external environment.

6. *From a state in which the nature of the core activities (achieving the objectives, maintaining the internal system, and adapting to the environment) is largely determined by the present to a state in which the present core activities are continually influenced by considerations including the past history, the present, and the anticipated future of the organization.*[16]

This dimension assumes that the axiologically good organization will be able to take into account, in defining its core activities, the relevant variables from the past and in the present, as well as to anticipate correctly the relevant variables of the future.

It will be a matter of empirical research to determine the appropriate time perspective for each organization.[17] One theo-

---

[16] The dimension could be considered a part of dimension 4. However, it is hypothesized that this degree of differentiation will help the model be operationally more useful.

[17] Elliott Jaques has provided some stimulating analyses regarding this problem. Some of these are discussed in subsequent chapters, see *Measurement of Responsibility* (Cambridge: Harvard University Press, 1956).

retical criterion of the "right" time perspective may be that amount of time necessary to solve a problem while at the same time optimizing dimensions 1, 2, 3, 4, and 5. Another criterion for determining the scope of the time perspective would be the amount of time that the organization needed to plan ahead to combat external stimuli.

MUTUAL DEPENDENCE OF DIMENSIONS

These are the dimensions that we hypothesize to represent states of affairs ranging from complete congruence to complete antagonism to the axiologically good organization. It is important to emphasize that each dimension is conceived to be mutually dependent on the other dimensions. A change in any one dimension, in any direction, under a given set of conditions will tend to influence the other dimensions. Exactly what these influences are, how they operate, and how any given one or subset of dimensions covaries with any other given one or subset of dimensions needs to be discovered through systematic empirical research. It may be, for example, that a change in dimension 1 going toward the axiologically good organization will influence the remaining dimensions differently, depending on their state (i.e., their position on each continuum). Clearly, the number of possible combinations is so large and the relationships so dynamically interrelated that we must wait for systematic empirical research to make explicit the interrelationships among the dimensions.

We now have a model with which to ascertain the degree to which any given empirical organization (individual or social) approximates the axiologically good or not-good organization. We are still far away, however, from providing the administrator with useful administrative insights. The fact that his organization may be an empirical example of some degree of axiological goodness or not-goodness is no reason to compel him to consider changes. Perhaps it is the organization that tends toward the axiologically not-good that is, from his viewpoint, the most efficient and effective.

THE ROLE OF ORGANIZATIONAL OBJECTIVES

The reader may wonder about the role that goal achievement plays in an axiologically good organization. This is an important point and one which unfortunately, because of lack of space, cannot be discussed in detail. Briefly, achieving organizational objectives is an important activity in an organization. However, based on our model, we would hypothesize a somewhat more restricted concept of goal achievement. An organization that approximates the axiologically good organization strives to achieve its objectives in such a way as to develop a profile on dimensions 1–6 that approximates as closely as possible the right ends of these continua.

Goal clarity, goal achievement, goal commitment—all factors that have been emphasized in the past—are, therefore, still considered important. The difference is that they are not enough. An axiologically good organization strives to achieve its goals in such a way that it is able to emphasize as much as possible the right ends of the continua on all the other dimensions.

Another way to state this is to hypothesize that *an organization should strive to achieve its objectives in such a way that it can maximize the probability that it will continue to achieve its objectives.* It is our hypothesis that the more the activities of the organization approximate the right ends of the continua, the greater the probability for continued goal achievement.

SOME USES OF THE MODEL

Let us pause for a moment to discuss several possible uses of the model. The first would be to provide the framework for a series of empirical descriptive studies of various kinds of organizations (e.g., prison, CIA, Red Cross, industrial plant, school, hospital, and church). Such studies could explore the possible relationships of various kinds of objectives and technologies to the dimensions of our model. It may be that prisons, in order to accomplish their objectives, must direct their activities toward the axiologically not-good organization and churches toward the axiologically good organization. Or we may find that churches and prisons are similar and that the same may be true for schools and industrial plants.

A somewhat related project would be to study the consequences to the organizations when their activities represented directions toward the axiologically good and when they were toward the axiologically not-good organization.

The studies, in turn, could lead to a third set of questions. One might conceive of these dimensions as "performance criteria" and ascertain how effectively a given organization "performed" in terms of these dimensions. For example, one organization might be found to attempt to maximize dimensions 1, 2, and 3 and minimize dimensions 3, 4, and 5. Another might do the opposite.

These three sets of studies are descriptive and do not entail normative issues. They attempt to relate empirical reality to a model. There is another set of studies, however, that imply normative values which may also be explored with the use of the model.

The first of these may be studies that ask how an organization is able to maximize the amount of human commitment for work that its participants are willing to manifest. The same studies could explore the mechanisms by which an organization can be structured to enhance the flexibility, openness, trust, and self-responsibility of its participants. Anyone who is acquainted with the concerns of administrators is aware of the importance of these factors. Interestingly, the same factors of self-responsibility, work (in the Bion sense), flexibility, openness, and trust are also characteristics of positive mental health and effective interpersonal relationships (Jahoda). As we shall see in a moment, Jahoda's conception of positive mental health is consonant with the state of affairs represented by the axiologically good organization.

Accepting the above as valid, for the moment, we may then hypothesize that it may be possible to integrate individual needs with organizational demands. The model may be of help in making explicit the requirements necessary if the integration of the individual and the organization is to occur.

In considering this type of question, we are leaving the axiologically good and beginning to move toward the normative good. We are implying that it is good to integrate the individual with the organization. A normative good may be defined as a personal command that individuals are willing to obey. One way to develop insight into the normative good is to postulate a command, accept it tentatively, and then spin out its consequences with respect to human actions.[18]

I should like to postulate that the individual ought to be valued and integrated in an organization and then attempt to spin out the consequences for the organization and for the individual. May I remind the reader that I am *not* suggesting that he should value the individual and his integration with the organization. I am simply asking him to go along with the hypotheses to see what human actions would be required if such a value were to be held.

THE NATURE OF THE INDIVIDUAL MENTAL HEALTH

Organizations develop their energies for decision making, creativity, and productivity from the people who "man" their roles, machines, committees, etc. If one examines the literature, one finds that man's motivation is conceptualized primarily in energy terms.[19] Human beings are assumed to manifest psychological energy as well as physiological energy.

[18] Henry Margenau, "The Scientific Basis of Value," in Abraham Maslow (ed.), *New Knowledge in Values* (New York: Harper & Bros., 1959).

[19] There is an increasing trend toward viewing man's actions in terms of cognitive information theory. I believe that the consequences which will be spelled out are the same, no matter how individual motivation is conceptualized. See Donald W. Taylor, "Toward an Information Processing Theory of Motivation," in *Nebraska Symposium on Motivation* (ed. Marshall R. Jones) (Lincoln: University of Nebraska Press, 1960), pp. 51–79, and George Kelley, *Psychology of Personal Constructs.*

Each kind of energy is interrelated with the other but is governed by its own laws. Focusing on the psychological energy, Reusch and Bateson,[20] and Rappaport and Gill[21] suggest the major properties assigned to this concept to be

1. It exists
2. It cannot be blocked
3. It varies with the state of mind of the individual

This means that, as the state of mind becomes "better," the individual should have more psychological energy available for work (in the genotype sense).[22] But what is a good state of mind? If we assume that a good state of mind is consonant with (if not isomorphic to) mental health, then we arrive at an interesting finding. The state of individual mental health as it is currently conceptualized by psychologists and psychiatrists is consonant with the axiologically good organization. For example, if one examines the Jahoda review of the literature, one may find in her book such statements as the healthy, flexible individual has access to all the parts of his experience and of his self.[22a] The rational ego is not constantly in authoritarian control but at appropriate times relinquishes control to the id or the superego (Kris's "voluntary regression" in service of the ego). The healthy individual functions as a totality which is controlled and created through the interrelationships of all the relevant parts of his self. He is aware of the pattern of parts and is able to influence his adjustment and adaptation as he finds it necessary. This implies that he is capable of effective problem solving. Thus the psychologically healthy individual strives to be self-responsible, self-directed, self-motivated, aspires toward excellence in problem solving, to decrease his defensive and complusive behavior, to be fully functioning, etc.

---

[20] J. Ruesch and G. Bateson, *Communication: The Social Matrix of Psychiatry* (New York: W. W. Norton & Co., 1951), pp. 248–49.

[21] David Rapaport and Merton Gill, "The Points of View and Assumptions of Metapsychology," *International Journal of Psycho-Analysis,* Vol. XL, Parts III–IV (·1959), pp. 1–10.

[22] W. R. Bion, "Experience in Groups," *Human Relationships,* Vol. I (1948), pp. 314 and 487–96.

[22a] Marie Jahoda, *Current Concepts of Positive Mental Health* (New York: Basic Books, Inc., 1958).

Kubie,[23] Fromm,[24] and Rogers[25] are three examples of scholars who believe that individual mental health, not neuroticism, is the deepest source of creativity. However, this does not say that a psychologically healthy individual *will* be productive and creative. It simply makes an assertion about his capability. In order for the capability to become an actuality, the organization will have to create a milieu, an environment, that encourages the expression of individual health.

As I suggested at the beginning, the typical formal organization, administrative controls, and directive leadership may tend to inveigh against individual mental health and induce individuals either to aspire toward dependency, submissiveness, etc., or to create informal activities that lead them to become apathetic, indifferent, and eventually alienated; these states, according to Jahoda, may lead to mental illness.

Elsewhere I have also suggested that these individual states of affairs feed back to create serious organizational difficulties that could lead to the deterioration of the organization. For example, as individuals increase their apathy and indifference, they also tend to increase their gold bricking, rate setting, cheating, requesting increased material rewards almost regardless of the financial state of the organization, and demanding programs that guarantee their job security. As these conditions increase, organizations can become so rigid and inflexible that they are unable to meet the competitive challenges of the present type of socioeconomic system under which they are operating.[26] Moreover, again as a function of the structure and

---

[23] Lawrence Kubie, *Neurotic Distortion of the Creative Process* (Lawrence: University of Kansas, 1958).

[24] Erich, Fromm, "The Creative Attitude," in Harold H. Anderson (ed.), *Creativity and Its Cultivation* (New York: Harper & Bros., 1959), pp. 44–54.

[25] Carl R. Rogers, "Toward a Theory of Creativity," in Harold H. Anderson (ed.), *Creativity and Its Cultivation* (New York: Harper & Bros., 1959), pp. 69–82.

[26] Chris Argyris, "The Organization, What Makes It Healthy," *Harvard Business Review*, Vol. XXXVI, No. 6 (November–December, 1958), pp. 107–17; and "Organizational Effectiveness under Stress," *ibid.*, Vol. XXXVIII, No. 3 (May–June, 1960), pp. 137–46.

the controls, management will tend to be placed in a situation wherein their interpersonal competence will decrease, while mistrust of themselves as well as of the employees, conformity, and dependence will tend to increase. These, in turn, will tend to have important negative impacts on rational decision making and simultaneously increase the practice of "management by crisis," as well as interdepartmental rivalries and rigidities. All these factors will tend to create an organization that will require increasing increments of inputs to obtain the same or decreasing increments of outputs. In the present socioeconomic milieu, this would eventually mean serious difficulties.

Perhaps it is now clear that I am trying to make the point that, as long as complex organizations use people, it may be possible that they will tend to obtain greater commitment, flexibility, responsibility, and openness and thereby enhance their chances for survival and growth if they strive to create conditions wherein the individual is able to actualize his potential as much as possible. More specifically, this would require organizations that attempted to structure themselves to increase the probabilities that the individuals would tend to:

a) Experience the wholeness of the organization
b) Be required to be self-responsible, self-directed, self-motivated
c) Aspire toward excellence in problem solving
d) Strive to decrease compulsive behavior and organizational defenses and increase the degree to which they can control their own environment
e) Utilize their abilities, especially their cognitive and their interpersonal abilities
f) Increase their time perspective

If one compares these organizational requirements with the axiologically good organization, one will find again that they are consonant. We conclude that a first step toward integrating the individual and the organization is for both to aspire toward the conditions represented by the axiologically good organization.

There may be another reason why an organization may want to consider enhancing the opportunities for individual selfactualizations. This is related to the new computer technology being developed. Computers will help organizations obtain more data, faster and more effectively, than ever before. This can have fascinating impacts on the organization and the human relationships within it. For example, in a recent study I found that relatively incompetent executives could hide their limitations (especially in taking risks and making decisions) because they could rationalize that "no one could possibly have enough of the relevant facts to make a decision." With the use of the computer, the number of facts that they could consider was greatly increased. So was their anxiety about making decisions. Their fear of taking risks and failing now came out into the open.

In another case the computer was placed on "real time," which meant that it would be used as an operating arm of the business. Before the use of the computer, it took 3–4 weeks before the president received feedback about the way certain decisions were implemented. Actually, it took about 2–3 weeks for the information to get to the vice-presidents. They would then "sit" on the results or, depending on the kind of results available, ask for a meeting with the president. If the results were not as good as expected, the vice-presidents spent several busy days "politicking" with one another in order to "soften" the feedback to be given the president. With the advent of the computer, it became possible for the president to receive the necessary information in 2–3 days. This pleased him, because, as he put it, "I'll now be able to nail things down and find out who are the real culprits." The same possibility created a new panic among the vice-presidents. As one remarked, "I simply won't have the time to politic anymore." Another worried because, as he put it, "Having this damn computer on real time means that there has to be a hell of a lot of trust, confidence, and leveling among people." In short, computers may well provide a new, a more urgent, stimulus for developing effective human relationships among the executives.

Another reason why the advent of computers may coerce

administrators to consider more seriously providing the individual with greater opportunity for self-actualization is related to the new search activities that will be possible with computers. One reason why the pyramidal structure has been useful in the past is that it was difficult to accumulate and feed to all parts of the organization the information necessary to explore alternatives and to make decisions. Consequently, the information was sent primarily to the leader. Now, however, it may be possible to involve more of the relevant people in searching for alternatives, as well as in developing final solutions. This will tend to require effective group functioning. In short, the computer has tremendous potential. However, it is primarily a tool. As such, it will probably be used to emphasize the values that the administrators desire. Again, our model may become of value. The administrator may have studies conducted to see the differential impact on the organization of various uses of computers.

Returning to our main theme, it is important to emphasize that we have oversimplified our problem. There are some nasty problems involved in achieving the integration of the individual and the organization that we have not made explicit. For example, there are times when the organization's requirements and the individual's needs will not be congruent. One will have to suffer if the other is to survive. At times the organization may have to "give in"; at other times the individual. But this is not a new problem to man. This is part of the basic process of becoming a fully functioning member in society.

To make matters more difficult, as was pointed out previously, the foregoing dimensions are highly dynamic and mutually dependent. For example, an organization may attempt to enhance its problem solving by bringing in staff groups, such as operations researchers. To the extent that these groups succeed, they will tend to decrease the employees' experience of the whole organization and increase the degree to which the staff may dominate the whole. Much research is going to be necessary to discover the precise relationships among the dimensions.

SUMMARIZING UP TO THIS POINT

We have suggested a series of interrelated dimensions based on the essential properties of organizations. We have concluded (1) that the axiologically good organization is consonant with individual mental health; (2) that individual mental health is positively associated with the capacity or potentiality (not the actuality) for the individual to produce, to be committed, creative, flexible; and (3) that the existence of these factors will tend to enhance the organization's capacity to achieve its objectives, survive, and perhaps develop.

But we have also said that it is not possible to create an organization wherein the individual needs and the organizational demands are completely consonant. The integration of the individual and the organization will never be perfect. We shall always be faced with the problem of compromise or "satisficing" (to quote Herbert Simon).

Hopefully, the value of the model that we are suggesting is that it may provide a systematic scheme with which to explore the problem of compromise or the processes of "satisficing." For example, perhaps it might be possible to conduct a series of studies utilizing the model to ascertain the consequences (costs and outputs) of various profiles. One study could focus on an organization whose profile approximated the axiologically not-good, one whose profile was at the center, and one whose profile approximated the axiologically good organization. The study could provide us with insights into the costs, as well as the outputs, of each profile. Such data could then be used by the participants of an organization to help them decide which profile they preferred to develop for their own organization.

The model, therefore, does *not* tell us what is a good organization. Rather, it provides a systematic procedure by which human beings can make more informed decisions about the form and character that their organizations shall take. *They,* not the researcher, decide the "oughts" in their life.[27]

---

[27] It may be useful to point out that the model is theoretically valid for any unity that is an organization, i.e., the individual, small group, large organization—indeed, for an entire society.

I should like to conclude this section with some speculations about an organization that is attempting to approximate, as closely as possible, the right ends of the continua (i.e., the axiologically good organization), I select this alternative (1) because a major emphasis of my research is to understand problems of individual mental health in industrial organizations and (2) because of the belief that enhanced individual health can lead to greater probabilities for organizational survival and growth.

Elsewhere, I hope, however, to consider other alternatives (e.g., where the individual is primarily neglected), in order to spell out, understand, and gain fuller understanding of organizational phenomena.

THE NATURE OF ORGANIZATIONAL LEADERSHIP

In discussing leadership, I am not focusing on the particular patterns of leadership that individuals tend to manifest as a result of their personality interacting with, and transacting upon, the situational context. I am not focusing on whether a particular leader does or should behave "democratically," "participatively," "autocratically," etc. This *is* an important dimension to be considered in planning the total changes to be made. However, because of time and space limitations, I should like to focus on the prescribed leadership roles—on the organizational policies and strategies—that an organization may develop and then require particular individuals to fulfill. I should like to focus on the requirements that an organization would make of all its executives as distinct from their personal leadership patterns.

The changes required of leaders in an organization will have to be very gradual. Consequently, I shall discuss the strategy for changes in organizational leadership in terms of successive stages. I know almost nothing regarding how long it will take to place each stage in practice. I know even less concerning how long it will take to develop all the stages in an organization. All that I am certain of is that it will probably take, as a minimum, several years and that the changes will be a function of a complex cluster of variables.

Stage I. *Reality-Centered Leadership*

Elsewhere, I tried to show that leadership research exhibited some important trends regarding what was considered to be "effective" leadership. It began by considering directive, firm "headship" leadership as most effective. With the onset of the Lewin, Lippitt, and White leadership studies, democratic leadership became the desired pattern for effective leadership by many practitioners. Democratic leadership was modified by various researchers to "participative," "collaborative," "employee-centered," "group-centered," etc., leadership.

In the same work, I try to defend the position that no one leadership style is the most effective. Each is probably effective under a given set of conditions. Consequently, I suggest that effective leaders are those who are capable of behaving in many different leadership styles, depending on the requirements of reality, as they and others perceive it. I call this leadership "reality-centered" leadership.[28]

The first step recommended is that the leaders be assisted to develop reality-centered leadership patterns. When a leader is reality-centered, he is able to diagnose a given administrative situation from the point of view of all those involved (including himself). We know from perceptual, clinical, and social psychology that diagnosing reality from many different individuals' points of view is quite difficult. It requires, among other things, a high degree of self-awareness, awareness of one's impact upon others, and awareness of their impact on oneself. It also requires a low degree of defensiveness in order (1) that one may admit to his cognitive field as many different factors as are relevant in the specific administrative situation and (2) that one can differentiate himself (his needs, anxieties, etc.) from the situation, thereby distorting less his perception—or at least being aware of his distortions.[29]

[28] See my *Personality and Organization* (New York: Harper & Bros., 1957), pp. 205–8.

[29] The latter ability is similar to what Rollo may have defined as being objective (i.e., to be aware of one's subjectivity). For an interesting article regarding the dynamics of "separating" the situation from oneself see Thomas S. Szasz, "The Communication of Distress between Child and Parent," *British Journal of Medical Psychology*, Vol. XXXII, Part 3 (1959), pp. 161–70.

Once the administrative situation is understood correctly, the leader must behave appropriately. *But what is appropriate behavior?* The probability is high that different leadership patterns will be appropriate for different situations. For example, under certain conditions "participative" leadership may be most effective. Under other conditions a more directive or laissez-faire leadership may be required.

It is therefore the responsibility of every executive in the organization considering any of these major organizational changes to develop his competence in several leadership patterns, so that he is able to shift from one to another with minimal ambiguity and personal insecurity. The leader must have his philosophy of leadership so well thought through, so internalized, and his competence in each leadership pattern so high that he will not tend to feel insecure or guilty when he changes his behavior from being directive to participative, etc. Moreover, it will be necessary for the leader to communicate clearly to the subordinates the conditions under which he will tend to behave in each given leadership style. This could be accomplished by developing a set of decision rules that made it operationally clear to the subordinates when he would use each of the different leadership patterns.

These requirements assume that it is possible for a leader to vary his leadership style according to the situation in which he exists. I believe this assumption to be congruent with the Jahoda model of mental health. A healthy individual, according to Jahoda, is able, among other things, to perceive reality accurately and can behave in such a way as to facilitate his and others' effectiveness in a given situation. The healthy individual also understands the reality requirements that are necessary if his society is to exist. He is not threatened by the environmental demands if he feels they are justified. If these characteristics of a healthy individual are valid, then reality-centered leadership is also valid. In fact, it seems that an effective leader is a healthy individual.

In the first stage, the leader behavior is consonant with the formal organizational strategy. He is in complete control. In

Lewin's terms he is the "keeper of the gate" through which the subordinates must pass if they are to achieve their goals and fulfill their needs. There is no basic shift in the flow of authority, rewards and penalties, and information. In the first stage, the leader is required to realize that administrative situations are complex and that they probably call for varying types of leadership patterns. From the subordinates viewpoint, if this stage is developed successfully, although he will still feel dependent and subordinate, the hypothesis is that he will tend to feel more understood.

In terms of our model, the leadership behavior reflects the "not-good" (axiologically) organization because the leader (one part) is primarily in control, he is primarily aware of the total problem (because he has the information), he directs the problem. However, such leadership may well help to achieve the organization's objectives.

Stage II. Subordinates and the Leader Control the Decision Rules for the Appropriate Leadership

The second stage is characterized by the leader's inviting the subordinates to participate with him in defining the decision rules that will guide him in his selection of a leadership pattern to use under specfically defined conditions. The participation in these deliberations is on the basis that each subordinate and the leader have equal power. The decision rules defined by the group will have to be accepted by them by consensus. Once the group has defined and accepted the decision rules, the leader can, if he wishes, disband the group. Any future modifications can be made by him and communicated to the subordinates.

A natural sequence to the above would be to offer to the subordinates permanent control over the definition of the decision rules. In giving control over the decision rules to the subordinates, the leader does not relinquish his freedom to decide how he shall behave in a particular leadership pattern. He is still in control over his style of leadership.

The organization is now beginning to require the leader to behave in ways that will increase the control of the subordinates over their world. Their awareness of the parts and the whole will tend to increase, as will their ability to influence the internally, as well as the externally, oriented core activities of the organization. Finally, they will begin to participate in, and begin to feel some responsibility for, the problem-solving process.

Stage III. The Subordinates and the Leader Control the Criteria Used to Reward and Penalize Them

In Stage III, we begin to modify the very nature of formal organizational leadership by beginning to alter the control over the organizational rewards and penalties. Under the pyramid organizational strategy the leader is responsible for defining the criteria by which salaries, promotions, demotions, etc., will be distributed. These are crucial variables in causing dependence and submissiveness on the part of a subordinate to a superior.

In Stage III the leader delegates to the subordinates the power to define the criteria that he will use to reward and penalize them. The leader will be permitted to participate fully in these deliberations. He will have one vote during the deliberations and thus be free to press for whatever viewpoint he desires. The decision will be one of consensus. Once the criteria are defined, the leader will be bound to use them. The leader can disband the group, once these criteria are defined. A natural sequence is to offer the subordinates permanent control over the re-examination and redefinition of the criteria. Again the leader will have only one vote, and the decisions must be reached by consensus. As in Stage II, the leader does not relinquish the power to do the actual rewarding and penalizing of the subordinates.

Stage IV. The Subordinates and the Leader Control the Use of the Rewards and Penalties

During the fourth stage the leader and the subordinates will share equally the control over the reward and penalty activities. The salaries, promotions, bonuses, etc., will now be under the control of the entire group. The rewards and penalties cannot be distributed without the authorization of all the individuals involved.

In the case of material rewards, such as money and benefits, it would be possible for the executive committee or the board to define the financial limits within which each department must work. For example, the department could be alloted $100,000 for their salaries. The exact distribution of these monies among the managers in the department would be the complete responsibility of the managers. In other words, I am not recommending that the managers tell the organization exactly how much they should earn. The organization would still be represented by the broad allocations which, presumably, set realistic limits (in the eyes of the owners or the board of directors) for the members of a particular department.

Stage V. The Subordinates and the Leader Control the Rules for Membership in the Make-up of the Group

The final change in leadership will be to give the subordinates, as well as the formal leader, control over the membership and make-up of the group. Research has shown that members value more highly those groups in which membership status is constantly reviewed and in which they participate and consequently have some control or influence.

The effect of introducing these stages will be, I believe, gradually to decrease the degree of dependence and subordination of the subordinates upon the leader. It should decrease the leader-centeredness, leader-dependence, the rivalry among subordinates, competition for the favor of the leader, and the tendency to evolve scapegoats.[30]

This decrease, in turn, should increase the probability that the subordinates can express themselves more freely, increase their sense of psychological success, and decrease their interpersonal competition, rivalry, and conflict. Such a state not only will tend to enhance the decision-making processes of the organization but will also tend to free the formal leader to

[30] Chris Argyris, *Executive Leadership* (New York: Harper & Bros., 1953).

consider problems of a longer-range nature for which previously he could not find the time.

In terms of our model of organizational health, the participants will experience a greater sense of interdependence with themselves and the whole. Their awareness, therefore, of the whole will tend to enlarge. Their capacity to modify their organization's (department's, group's, etc.) internal make-up will increase. Their time perspective will also be enlarged.

If we examine the direction of the organizational changes, in terms of our model, they all lead to activities that will reflect the axiologically good organization. Thus the members will become increasingly aware of the whole organization. Also, the members will have a greater influence on how the whole is created and maintained internally, as well as how it adapts to its external environment. Finally, they will have a greater voice in significant problem-solving activities, as well as greater organizational freedom to say what they really feel on important questions in which they do not make the final decisions. These conditions will, in turn, tend to create a milieu in which the individuals will be required to develop increasingly along the Jahoda dimensions of positive individual mental health. For example, the individuals will experience a greater responsibility for their and their fellow employees' future, a longer time perspective, a greater opportunity for psychologically challenging activities, ego-involvement, etc.

One word of warning. These organizational changes cannot be induced by edict. These changes, especially the last two stages, require a very high degree of interpersonal trust and openness, as well as a deep sense of caring among the participants. The changes also require the development of a fully functioning and well-integrated group. The most important reason for a group is that it can optimize the uniqueness of the individual members, thereby creating a milieu in which the individual contributes to the best of his ability. A fully functioning, well-integrated group does not develop easily—certainly not any more easily than the development of a fully functioning, integrated individual.

In a recent study I found that interpersonal competence,

trust, openness, and experimentation, as well as an effective group, can begin to be developed by the use of the "laboratory approach." I am persuaded that if the laboratory method is used properly, it can be a powerful tool to help an organization develop toward the states of affairs characterized by the axiologically good organization, as well as toward the dimensions of Jahoda's positive mental health. In saying this I am not suggesting that the laboratory approach is, or involves, individual or group therapy that hopefully helps individuals resolve their neurotic or psychotic difficulties.[30a]

The point that I should like to make is that unless the participants deeply believe in and are able to behave in a manner consistent with the values implicit in an axiologically good organization and Jahoda's dimensions of positive mental health, all the changes suggested above in the nature and use of organizational leadership will fail because they will be perceived by the subordinates for what they really are: gimmicks and techniques to manipulate people and techniques that place power in the hands of people who do not tend to trust one another or probably themselves.

THE NATURE OF ORGANIZATIONAL STRUCTURE

Although leadership may be the first to be changed, it must never be forgotten that it operates within an organizational structure. Let us now turn our attention to some possible modifications in the organizational structure of modern formal organizations.

Before the modifications are presented, I should like to state two working hypotheses. First, a reminder about the nature of any organizational structure. Organizational structures are *strategies* designed to achieve specific objectives. The structure of the organization is a snapshot or static picture of the dynamics of the strategy being used. From our point of view, a strategy that optimizes the organizational core activities of achieving the objectives, maintaining the organization, and adapting to the environment is the best strategy. The present

---

[30a] Chris Argyris, *Interpersonal Competence and Organizational Effectiveness,* to be published by Richard D. Irwin, Inc. and The Dorsey Press, Inc., 1962.

formal organizational strategy assumes that individual self-actualization is not relevant for the effectiveness of the core activities. Our analysis suggests that the effectiveness of the core activities is highly influenced by the degree of individual self-actualization. Therefore, some new strategies must be invented and applied if the effectiveness of the core activities is to be maximized.

The second working hypothesis is that I assume in this analysis that no new organizational strategy will be devised in the foreseeable future that will, or should, completely supplant the old formal strategy. The pyramidal strategy has survived and for important reasons. There may be times that the survival of the organization will require a strategy to be used that is based on centralization of power, control, and specialization. For example, in cases of emergency, when the time necessary for adequate participation by the agents of the organization is not available, the pyramidal strategy may be very effective for routine decisions. There are hundreds of decisions made daily in an organization that do not require the participation of more than one individual. Finally, a certain degree of specialization for technological tasks seems effective. To the extent that this is true, the pyramidal strategy would probably be most effective.

There may be other times when the survival of the organization would require that the emphasis be placed on the individuals. Still other times, the emphasis may be upon certain groups or some other subunity within the larger whole. Therefore, as in the case of leadership, there is no one single organizational strategy that is best for all decisions. *The organization of the future will vary the strategy it uses and thus its structure according to the kinds of decisions that it faces.*

A central task for organization planning in the future will be to discover new organizational strategies and to make explicit the conditions under which (i.e., under what types of decisions) they may be used. The objective below is to discuss in a most exploratory manner four different organizational strategies and the conditions under which each may be used most appropriately. It is emphasized that we are suggesting that all four structures should operate in a given organization.

1. The Use of Formal Organizational Strategy

One may hypothesize the following conditions under which the formal organizational strategy may be used:

a) When the time available for a decision to be made is less than that which would be required for the relevant information (1) to flow to all the relevant parts of the organization, (2) to be discussed, and (3) a decision to be made.

If a customer asks for an increase in his order or immediate delivery and promises to cancel the entire order if his wishes are not met, the organization will probably desire to make that decision quickly and at the immediate point of contact with the customer (e.g., sales organization). Another example is if an emergency arises and the organization's survival is threatened if immediate action is not taken. Still another example may be the decision to buy some raw materials at low prices if one moves within a specified time limit.

b) When the information relevant to the decision is understandable by and/or available to only a few individuals.

If the organization wants to decide whether a particular raw material is effective, whether a particular intricate mechanical process is useful, whether a particular investment is financially sound, it seems that the participants will want the individuals competent in these areas to cope with the issues.

One has to be careful in ascertaining what is understandable and available. In the case of the former, there are many cases on record where nonprofessional employees have helped to make highly technical decisions because they were close to the problems being discussed. Similarly, information may not be available at a particular point in the structure because the organization is so structured that information does not tend to flow to that point.

c) When a decision to be made falls clearly into a category which, as a result of prediscussion and agreement among the participants, has been relegated to the formal organizational structure.

Participants may decide that there are certain classes of decisions in which they should not be included. These decisions will be those that require minimal commitment on the part of the participant. They will be decisions that require little or no use of the employees' motor, cognitive, or interpersonal abilities. Under these conditions the participants will not tend to see participation in the decision as relevant or necessary. Indeed, participation under these conditions might be costly in terms of time, energy, and money. Examples may be routine orders for products, delivery of raw materials to the line, routine requests about the disposition of orders, probable delivery dates, etc.

Another way of viewing this problem is that the formal strategy may be used when a decision must be made that does not significantly influence the distribution of power, rewards, penalties, information flow, and specialization of work. In other words, the changing of the organizational strategy used cannot be accomplished by edict from above.

Analyzing the conditions stated above, one finds that they include situations in which the participant can be rationally expected and required to be submissive without its influencing negatively his commitment to, and development within, the organization. For example, if the organization manufactures shoes, then one may assume that a committed employee will be glad to know that his firm is receiving orders or that a customer needs to be satisfied quickly. Also, one may assume that the participant's commitment is not negatively affected if decisions which he desires to be made without him are made without his participation. He realizes that he can be frustrated and, indeed, pressured if he is required to participate in making routine decisions or decisions that are clearly out of the range of his competence or involvement.

These are two fundamental assumptions underlying these statements. One is that man can be expected to be rational. The other is that man can be expected to be dependent and submissive. And thus I am back to the strategy of the original scientific management adherents. In my opinion, this is not incongruent with my primary thesis. All that I have done is to accept the importance of—indeed, the necessity for—human rationality and mutual dependence, but I have limited them to specific situations. In effect, I am suggesting that it is understandable for the organization to expect and require rationality and dependence on the part of its participants when the decision to be made is (1) to achieve an already accepted objective (e.g., producing and selling shoes), (2) to decide upon a matter within the competence of only a few employees, and (3) to decide upon a matter that the employees consider either routine or not significantly related to those factors that affect their commitment to the organization.

2. The Modified Formal Organization Structure

Rensis Likert and some of his associates have been developing an organizational structure that represents a move in the direction toward the axiologically good organization but is still based on the traditional formal organization structure. The traditional chain-of-command flow of information and controls are maintained for all crucial decisions, such as salaries, promotions, demotions, transfers, etc. The difference in this model from the traditional ones is that it conceives of any given superior as a *representative* of his *group's* (not only his own) view to the group of his peers and his boss. Under this structure the superior provides his subordinates an opportunity for true participation to voice their views on a particular matter. He then represents these views accurately to his peers and the executives above him. According to this model, the structure provides the subordinates an opportunity to experience greater satisfaction in and deeper commitments for the decisions made, since they participate significantly in these decisions.

In terms of our model, this structure should be most effective in decisions that require the individual's actualization to be taken into account but not as much as the organization's. In the case of conflict between individual and organizational need, the decision would probably have to be made in the interests of the firm. Another case would be when the opinions of all the participants is desired but with no opportunity made available to them to participate in the making of the decision. An example of the former may be the acceptance of a large order by management that may place much pressure on the organization in terms of meeting a deadline. Under these conditions, the management may decide to canvass the opinion of some of the participants, in order to gauge more accurately the impact of the new order. However, the actual decision to commit the organization may still be made by the management. An example of the latter case is when management is contemplating making new changes in the production processes and wishes to obtain the views of the employees regarding the changes. The management will listen to all the relevant views but it will make the final decision.

The Likert structure is ideal under these conditions because it permits individual participation with the possibility (if it should become necessary) for the top executive to override the decision made by the group and/or to go ahead and make his own decision without waiting for the group to decide.

Summarizing: one may hypothesize that the Likert strategy may be used:

a) When the decision is not routine but does not affect significantly or permanently the distribution of power, control, information, and the specialization of work (e.g., purchasing equipment, scheduling rush orders, establishing selling prices, etc.).

b) When adequate time is not available to include all the relevant individuals and/or to explore throughly the relevant issues. Adequate time *does* exist, however, to provide opportunities for participation of the upper-level executives (modifying selling arrangement, promising delivery dates, modifying delivery dates, etc.).

c) When the decision to make a major change cannot be delegated to all involved. However, participation is desired (from those affected by the change) in order to (1) decrease resistance to change, (2) develop the most effective processes for a lasting change within the organization, and (3) represent more adequately the needs of the participants involved in the change. The Coch and French studies and the Morse and Reimer studies are excellent examples of this approach. In the case of the former it was found that the experience of being allowed to participate in decisions usually reserved for management (the design of a new job, setting of the piece rates, etc.) increased the workers' effectiveness.[31] In the case of the latter, it was found that high control from above tended to reduce the effectiveness of work groups.[32]

The Likert strategy represents a step away from the formal organizational strategy, in that the views of subordinates are considered more systematically and—hopefully—more seriously. The strategy, however, does not alter significantly the basic flow of information, rewards and penalties, power, and authority. One may characterize it as an enlightened strategy embedded within, or subservient to, the pyramidal strategy. In some cases it has been used in an attempt to cover up or increase the control inherent in the pyramidal structure.

3. *Power According to Functional Contribution*

Under this strategy each individual has equal opportunity to be given power, controls, information, etc. The individual (individuals) is (are) given power as a function of his (their) potential contribution to the problem. For example, a company has a problem of putting into production a new product. A meeting is held in manufacturing with all levels (skilled workers, foremen, general foremen, superintendents, etc.). During the meeting it becomes apparent to the group that skilled Worker A, Foreman B, and General Foreman C are the most capable to engineer the new product. They are given the authority, etc., that they require to engineer the new product. Although the group members will work "under" these three "leaders," they may at any time meet as a group to consider change in the leadership. The power and control are, therefore, given to the individuals by the group members because they believe that the three individuals can lead the manufacturing department to its goals most effectively.

In short, any given subunit has the authority and responsi-

---

[31] Lester Coch and John R. P. French, Jr., "Overcoming Resistance to Change," *Human Relations*, Vol. I (1948), pp. 512–32.

[32] Nancy Morse and E. Reimer, "The Experimental Change of a Major Organizational Variable," *Journal of Abnormal and Social Psychology*, Vol. LII, No. 1 (1956), pp. 120–29.

bility to elect its own leadership, define its own controls, etc.,
for any given problem-solving activity. The individuals within
the subunit receive their power according to the members'
perception of their potential contribution to the core activities
(achieving the subunit's objective, maintaining itself internally, and adapting to the larger whole).[33]

Other examples of the kinds of decisions that such a structure
may be used are:

a). In the development of a new product it may be wise to
bring together to make the decisions those individuals who will
have to see to it that it becomes a success. These may include,
for example, product development engineering, manufacturing
sales, and finance, in order to evaluate the problems involved
in the new product, including introducing it into the market,
manufacturing, selling, distributing, and financing the new
product.

b) The solution of a problem involving more than one department or more than one individual within the department.
Ways to discover new cost and error and waste reduction may
be more effectively accomplished by bringing together the
individuals who must actually carry out these programs.

c) The organization's long-range policy-planning activities
may be more effective if they are conducted by all the participants in the organization. Not only may an organization gain
from the different points of view, but such participation will
tend to increase the commitment, that the individuals will have
to the long-range plans.

4. *Power According to Inevitable Organizational Responsibili- ties*

Under this structure each individual has equal power and
responsibility, and *he may not relinquish it.* It may be necessary to modify this to read, "unless there is a consensus decision

---

[33] This strategy was initially defined by Knickerbocker and McGregor, "The
Consultant Role and Organizational Leadership: Improving Human Relations
in Industry" (ed. D. McGregor), *Journal of Social Issues,* Vol. IV, No. 3
(Summer, 1948), pp. 2–40.

for all individuals to delegate their power and responsibility to one (or a few) individual(s)." Such a structure is used for those decisions in which maximum individual productivity and maximum feelings of responsibility and internal commitment are desired—for example, when a decision is to be made regarding promotions, salaries, or the acceptance of a departmental production objective. Under these conditions the desire will be to maximize individual participation in the decision-making activities and maximize the individual's commitment to carrying out his part of the decision and to help others do the same.

Other examples where such a structure may be used are:

a) The decision significantly affects the distribution of power, control, information, and the specialization of work.

b) The decision defines the rules that specify the conditions under which any one of the structures will be used.

c) The decision defines (for any given unit, subunit) the rules that specify the type of leadership to be used (see previous section).

d) The decision defines (for any given unit, subunit) the criteria for advancement, demotion, and other crucial rewards and penalties (see previous section).

e) The decision involves changing the nature of any of the core activities.

f) The decisions to define the content of and participate in any kind of activity designed to develop individuals.

As in the case of organizational leadership, the introduction of strategies 3 and 4 into an organization will require a long period of time to institute. The members of each unit will have to develop effective skills in group problem solving which will provide them the capability of developing groups that maximize the probability of individual internal commitment and responsibility toward himself, his fellow workers, and the organization. At this moment, few such groups exist in complex organizations.

Along with the development of effective skills for group decision making, the individuals will have to increase their self-awareness, self-trust, and their awareness and trust of others. These are required (1) if the individuals in the organizations are not to create "sick" groups in which the individual is required to conform and where it takes hours for decisions to be made and (2) if the individuals are to feel free to delegate their power to the individual they believe is the most effective leader for that particular decision. The leadership in the group will be shared among the members. Theoretically, the leadership, for any given decision, will be offered by the group members to the individual who, they consider, understands their desires and goals, is best capable of helping them to achieve the goals, and needs to perform the leadership function.

I have discussed four types of organizational structures and enumerated some of the conditions under which they may be used in an organization. I am assuming that an organization will use concurrently all four structures (and more, as others are constructed.) If one asks an individual in the organization of the future to see the company organizational chart, he would be asked "For what type of decision?"

It might also be emphasized that the task of defining the decision rules to tell the participants which organizational structure should be used under a given set of conditions would be assigned to as many participants as possible. In other words, although the organization would use at least one strategy that minimized individual self-actualization, formal organizational strategy was to be used in their organization. If autocracy was to be used, the use of it would be defined under participative conditions (structure 4). Control, in a given unity, over its core activities would be in the hands of as many individuals within that unity as possible.

In terms of our model, each organizational structure represents a step closer to the axiologically good organization and to the Jahoda dimensions of individual mental health. The closer one approximates organizational strategies 3 and 4, the greater the probability that the whole will be created and maintained by the interrelationship of parts (dimension 1);

there will be an awareness of a pattern of parts (dimension 2); the participants' ability to influence the internally and externally directed core activities will tend to increase (dimensions 3 and 4); the base and participation in problem solving will tend to increase (dimensions 5); and, finally, the probability will tend to increase that the relevant past and future will influence the present decision making (dimension 6).

At the same time, the participant's opportunity to use more of his abilities, to experience psychological involvement, internal commitment, and success, will tend to increase. Feelings of self-responsibility, identity, and essentiality may also tend to increase. In short, the individual will tend to find himself immersed in and working with several organizational strategies that will require that he aspire toward increasing increments of positive mental health. Under these conditions we are on our way to integrating the individual and the organization in such a way that both may gain from the integration.

SUMMARY AND CONCLUSIONS

1. The objective of this theoretical paper is to begin to explore the problems involved in attempting to integrate the individual and the organization.

2. The integration of the individual and the organization is so complex that it is doubtful whether it is possible to find maximum solutions. "Satisficing" solutions are probable.

3. In order to help us understand the problems of "satisficing," a model is developed that is composed of six interrelated dimensions.

4. The closer one approximates the right ends of the continua of the dimensions in the model, the greater the probability that the integration of the individual and the organization will tend to increase.

5. The model does *not* provide suggestions as to what is the "best" or "correct" organization for anyone to use. Rather it serves as a tool with which one may be able to evaluate the costs and outputs of different "profiles." The ultimate decision

for developing the form and character of the organization resides in the participants. Hopefully, the model may help them to develop more informed decisions.

6. The paper closes with some suggestions regarding organizational leadership and structure if someone were interested in integrating the individual and the organization.

3

THE CAREERS OF AMERICAN BUSINESS AND GOVERNMENT EXECUTIVES: A COMPARATIVE ANALYSIS

W. Lloyd Warner

INTRODUCTION: THE PRACTICAL AND SCIENTIFIC PROBLEMS

WE PEOPLE OF the United States, animated by equalitarian and aristocratic values and beliefs, both inherent and significant parts of this democracy, have always firmly voiced and attempted to practice equality of opportunity for everyone in our systems of rank. This means in practical terms that every person during his or her career must be able to get a job and during the working lifetime, should abilities and skills permit, advance to higher positions of prestige and power. We believe that men from all economic ranks, those born to low or high position, with the necessary ability, talent, and training, merit the rewards of occupational advancement. Moreover, in our value system not only is this just and right for the individuals involved, but, to make our competitive, economic, and social system work, we believe that in the competition for the most important jobs the best men should win.

Our prevailing fears about ourselves and our society reinforce these more positive feelings about equality of opportunity just stated. Many believe that this condition of equality no longer prevails; large numbers of our population are of the firm opinion that there is less opportunity today than previously for men born to low station to climb to the top. They also are convinced that the social and economic hierarchies of America are growing more rigid, are less open and more closed to the advance of the talented and trained who come from the lower levels of this society. Much of the literature of the social sciences, sociology particularly, especially during the 1930's and 1940's, emphasized the pessimistic side of this important question.

In this chapter I shall report on two extensive researches conducted by my colleagues and myself that were designed to find some of the answers to a number of the more significant questions about this important practical and scientific problem. The men who occupy the highest positions in big business throughout the United States were first studied.[1] Those who hold the highest positions of authority in the federal government were then examined.[2] Comparisons were made and conclusions drawn about the amount of movement in each hierarchy. Since the concentrations of power and prestige in business and government include a large proportion of the most powerful and prestigeful positions in the occupational structure of this country, they both provide a factual demonstration of what present reality is and are probable indexes of the general fluidity and rigidity of our society. They help answer questions about the amount of equality of opportunity there is for men of all ranks in the United States.

Before turning to the research results, I shall briefly review the basic questions we asked of our evidence and present the methods and techniques used. We first asked, Who are the

---

[1] W. L. Warner and J. C. Abegglen, *Occupational Mobility in American Business and Industry* (Minneapolis: University of Minnesota Press, 1955), and *Big Business Leaders in America* (New York: Harper & Bros., 1955).

[2] W. L. Warner, P. P. Van Riper, N. H. Martin, and O. F. Collins, *The American Federal Executive,* to be published by Yale University Press, 1962.

big business and big government leaders of America? What
kinds of men are they? Do they come from all occupational
levels in equal proportions? Are most of these men of big
business and high executive authority in the federal government from the elite classes, or do some come in significant proportions from the lower ranks, from the manual workers and
white-collar levels and other more modest occupations?
Scientifically speaking, the extent to which they are the sons of
big businessmen and high government officials is, of course,
the extent to which the American society is closed and not
open to free competition; it is the degree to which our collectivity is rigid and emphasizes aristocratic principles rather
than democratic ones. The extent to which movement takes
place from the bottom to the top and from the intermediate
levels in these two great hierarchies is a measure of free competition, of a more flexible society, and of a social and occupational system of open statuses.

For those concerned with the political domain and the
domestic well-being of the body politic as conceived by Thomas
Jefferson and Samuel Adams, we can ask and answer other important questions: Do we have a truly representative government insofar as these federal executives are concerned? Are
the men at the very top levels of the federal government representative of the varieties of men and women who compose all
walks of life in the American collectivity? Or are they a special
group who represent the few (in terms of who they are) and
not the many?

Comparisons between these studies and earlier ones on these
two elites of previous generations, particularly those on big-
business leaders,[3] give us reliable answers about trends in the
comparative rigidity and fluidity of our occupational structure. Comparisons between the civilian government executives
and the big-business leaders yield exact statements about the
equality of opportunity in government and business.

---

[3] F. W. Taussig and C. S. Joslyn, *American Business Leaders* (New York:
Macmillan Co., 1932)

Let us briefly define the meanings of business and government executives before we discuss them further. We shall do this operationally. Only big-business leaders who held the highest policy-making positions were selected—those from chairman of the board and owner down only so far as secretary and treasurer. Only the largest corporations among the types of business enterprise, such as manufacturing, mining, finance, transportation, and the like, were chosen. The size of the corporation was defined in terms of the largest share of the gross national product in that category of enterprise. In brief, the big-business leaders were the biggest of their kind in this country.

For government executives, the military leaders ranged from admirals and generals down only to full colonels. For civilians, they ranged from the highest grade level (GS-18 and above) down to GS-14, these being positions of the very highest consequence in the federal government hierarchy. Only civilians are reported on here. Included were executives from the career civil service, those politically appointed, and the foreign service. There were 8,300 business leaders in our sample and approximately 13,000 government leaders. Our sample of each group by various tests proved to be representative and our evidence for each valid. We can, with this brief résumé of the method and purpose of the inquiry, turn to the results of the two studies.

THE SOCIAL AND ECONOMIC ORIGINS OF THE BUSINESS AND GOVERNMENT ELITES

The fundamental question we must first ask is: What were the occupational origins of the men of business and those of government? More precisely put—What were the occupations of their fathers, the economic positions of their families of birth? How many of the two elites came from the wrong side of the tracks? How many were born to high estate or to the more modest intermediate levels between the extremes? To obtain first answers let us turn to Table 1 for the comparative percentages for the executives of big business and government. The occupational origins of the executives of business and government are broadly alike, yet in many ways they vary rather dramatically. Table 1 lists nine major categories of occupation, running from major executives and owners of large business down the column through professional men, farmers, to unskilled laborers and farm laborers. To the right are the percentages and rank order for the occupations of the fathers of big-business leaders. The next columns list the occupations of the fathers of the civilian federal executives. It will be noticed that about one third (31 per cent) of the fathers of big-business leaders were also major executives or owners; a little more than half that many (18 per cent) were owners of small

TABLE 1

The Occupational Origins of Big-Business
and Federal Government Executives

	Business Leaders (Per Cent)	Rank Order	Federal Executives (Per Cent)	Rank Order
Major executive and owner of large business	31	1	17	2–3
Owner of small business	18	2	14	4–5
Foreman	3	8	5	7
Professional man	14	3	19	1
Clerk or salesman	8	6	9	6
Farmer	9	5	14	4–5
Skilled laborer	10	4	17	2–3
Unskilled laborer	5	7	4	8
Farm laborer	0	9	0	9
Others	2	..	1	..

business; a slightly smaller percentage (14 per cent) were professional men. Business leaders whose fathers were skilled laborers (10 per cent), farmers (9 per cent), and white-collar workers (8 per cent) fill the middle range in the rank order of fathers' occupations; those of the unskilled workers (5 per cent), foremen (3 per cent), and farm laborers (less than half of 1 per cent) were least represented. In general, the sons of men in occupations of higher position and prestige ranked first; those of moderate prestige came next; and the low-ranking occupations, as they are valued in this society, came in a poor third. For example, there were six times as many sons of higher executives and big-business leaders who themselves were big-business leaders (four times for government) than those who had fathers who were unskilled laborers. This spread in general, as we have seen, is true for both hierarchies.

A somewhat similar arrangement of government executives is revealed in the column to the right. The more highly placed professions and major executives ranked first and the least-valued occupations last. Yet the differences in the percentages of the two elites, government and business, are important, from the point of view both of scientific inquiry and of their meanings to our society. The sons of the major professions led all others (19 per cent) for government executives. The fathers who were big-business leaders (with 17 per cent) were second. Tied significantly with them were the sons of skilled laborers. They rose to 17 per cent, over their score for business leaders, and therefore ranked second. It will be noted that the sons of farmers rose to 14 per cent from 9 per cent for business leaders.

Given the two spreads of occupational percentage, we can now ask still more significant questions that will tell us more precisely about movement in the society and how the hierarchies of government and business compare in their emphasis on aristocratic and democratic values. The last analysis supplied evidence about the number of men who rose or who had been born to high position. We must now compare these figures with those for the occupations from the whole society, with a hundred and eighty million, to learn in what proportion the various occupations in our society are represented in the two elites. This, of course, will be a simple ratio. What occupations are over- and underrepresented and how much?

An exact measurement can be made by comparing the occupations of the fathers of the business and government leaders with the adult male population at the time these men started their careers. A perfect ratio, statistically speaking, would be 1:1, which means that the same percentage of a given occupation is found among the fathers of business and government leaders as in the general population. For example, if a third of the adult males in our occupational forces were laborers, then, to have an exact representation among government and business leaders, there should be a third of them from the laboring class. If we allow 100 to stand for perfect representation of the proportions between each of the samples and the general population, we can state the fact quite simply. All of this is represented in Table 2, called

TABLE 2

🎔 WHAT OCCUPATIONS GET "THEIR SHARE" IN GOVERNMENT AND BUSINESS?

Business Leaders Whose Fathers Were:		Federal Executives Whose Fathers Were:	
775	Executive or owner large business	567	Over
360	Owner small business	200	"Their
350	Professional man	475	Share"
133	Foreman	250	
100 = Neither above nor below their share			
80	Clerk or salesman	75	Under
63	Skilled laborer	113	"Their
45	Farmer	88	Share"
16	Unskilled laborer	12	
00	Farm laborer	00	

"What Occupations Get 'Their Share' in Government and Business?"

The nine occupations, beginning with major executives and running down to farm laborers, are found in the center of the table. At the left are the ratios for the business leaders whose fathers belonged to these different occupations. To the right are the fathers of the federal executives. Running laterally through the center of the page is the statement "100 = Neither above nor below their share," meaning that those figures that are above this are overrepresented for particular occupations and those under this line are below what might be expected by chance. We shall first examine the ratios of business leaders and start with the executives who are sons of big-business leaders. Four occupations are over what would be expected by chance among the business leaders. There are 775 sons of major executives or owners of large business for every 100 that would be there by chance. There are 360 for every 100 sons of small businessmen, some 350 sons of professional men, and 133 who had fathers who were foremen.

Among the federal executives, the distribution of ratios is somewhat similar, yet certain significant and important differences are present. The overrepresentation for the men who are sons of big businessmen drops to 567 for every 100 expected. Sons of professional men rise to 475. Those who are sons of foremen rise to 250, while the sons of owners of small business drop to 200. Down below 100, it will be noted among the big-business leaders that, for every 100 sons of skilled laborers that would be expected, there are but 63, a significant drop below expectancy, whereas for the federal executives there were 113 for every 100, a figure somewhat above expectancy. There are other significant differences among those occupations that are underrepresented between the two elites. For every 100 white-collar men, there are but 80 for businessmen and 75 for those in government. For every 100 farmers, there are but 45 among businessmen, but this figure about doubled with 88 for the government men. However, there are 16 sons of unskilled laborers among the businessmen and only 12 among the executives of the federal government. Broadly stated, the men of government are more representative of the general categories of occupation in our society than are big-business leaders. The overrepresentation tends to be not as great for the more highly placed occupations; on the other hand, the positions that are underrepresented and less valued in prestige tend to be somewhat more highly represented in government than in business. There is, however, the significant variation for the sons of unskilled laborers.

THE PROFESSIONS AS SOURCES OF FEDERAL EXECUTIVES

The broad categories of occupation that we have been using are for present purposes; it is impossible here to break them down into smaller, more precise subcategories. However, we can take time briefly to analyze one of the more interesting, that of professional men. The professions ranked high both for government and for business as sources of leadership.

The question arises: What professions led all others and what professions were most productive sources of government and federal executives? When one compares the proportions of the various professions between big-business leaders and the civilian federal executives, in many respects they look very much alike (Table 3). The ratios for the sons of lawyers are

TABLE 3

THE PROFESSIONS AS SOURCES OF GOVERNMENT
AND BUSINESS EXECUTIVES

Profession	Business Leaders	Federal Executives
Lawyer	800	844
Minister	548	667
Engineer	480	477
Doctor	478	595
Other professions	189*	274

* Includes: teachers, 224; College presidents and professors, 1,417.

almost identical. Ministers are second for big-business leaders as for civilian federal executives, but the latter ratio is larger. The proportions for engineers are almost exactly the same— 480 for business leaders and 477 for civilian federal executives. Doctors, however, ranked third for civilian federal executives —almost 600 for every 100 that might be expected by chance —and fourth for business—478, or approximately 500 for every 100 expected. The other professions, including teachers and professors, had a proportion of 189 for business leaders and 274 for civilian federal executives. (We did not derive separate ratios for teachers and professors for the business leaders as we did for government executives.)

The sons of professors were present in the civilian federal executive approximately fourteen times more than might be expected, outranking all other professional groups; among all the professions, teachers ranked last. Perhaps, as a point of interest, we might add that comparisons between the civilian federal executives and military leaders brings out a number of rather significant differences among the professions. The sons of lawyers, rather than the sons of professors, outrank all others among military leaders. Their representation is eleven times greater than would be expected from their proportions in the general population. These are followed by the sons of doctors, with nine times more than expected, and by professors, with 750 for every 100 expected. Teachers, for the military as for the civilian, among the professions were last.

THREE GENERATIONS OF MOBILITY IN BUSINESS AND GOVERNMENT

The analysis of the relations between the two generations, fathers and sons, brings out significant and important processes operating in our occupational structure as they are related to the top positions in the two powerful and prestigeful elites. We must now examine the problem from the vantage point of three generations. We can ask and answer the question, Do the two generations tell the complete story, or does the addition of a third generation, the grandparental one, add to our understanding of what occurs in the movement of personnel through the levels of occupation in our society? Because of the limitations of space, we shall present the evidence in summary form to bring out some of the more significant points about the meaning of three generations in the movement of people in and out of high position in business and government.

Without resorting to a long review of percentages and figures, we can briefly summarize the relation of the third generation to the occupational mobility of executives of business and industry. Perhaps the most significant comment that one can make is the tremendous change in proportions from

the fathers' to the grandfathers' generations insofar as farmers are involved (see Table 4). For example, over one third
of the fathers' fathers of the businessmen were farmers, and an
even higher percentage of the government men's grandfathers.
Their sons moved to the city, became laborers or white-collar
men, or moved into one of the other occupations in sizeable
numbers, this being true for all occupations except big business. Many of the laboring group of the third generation
tend to move up and to the white-collar class, insofar as the
populations of the two hierarchies are concerned. In general,

TABLE 4

THREE GENERATIONS OF OCCUPATIONAL MOBILITY

Occupation	Business (Per Cent)		Government (Per Cent)	
	Grandfather	Father	Grandfather	Father
Farmer	35	9	44	15
Laborer	19	15	18	21
Owner of small business	17	18	14	14
Major executive and owner of large business	12	24	6	10
Professional man	10	14	10	19
Minor executive	3	11	4	11
Clerk or salesman	2	8	3	9
Other	2	2	1	1

white-collar and the small-business categories are the embarka-
tion points for further mobility.

THE GOVERNMENT AND BUSINESS ELITES OF TODAY AND YESTERDAY: TRENDS OF MOBILITY AND OF EQUAL OPPORTUNITY

We have now arrived at the place where we can ask and, with
approximate accuracy, partly answer the questions, Is mobility
increasing or decreasing? Is the American society more open
today than yesterday? Or is it becoming more rigid and tending toward closure and inequality?

In 1928 Taussig and Joslyn made their important and authoritative study of American business leaders; to study

trends, the research of Warner and Abegglen in 1952 repli-
cated it. It is therefore possible, for the business leaders, to
make exact comparisons about the differences or similarities in
the amount of mobility between the generation of leaders one
generation ago and those of the present day. This is not possible for the government leaders, since no exact studies were
made of them at that time or earlier. However, a number were
made which do give indications of what has happened among
government executives; the results tend to parallel those of the
business leaders. Before continuing, it must be re-emphasized
that the operations of the 1928 study are the same as those for
the present-day business leaders. Furthermore, it should be
said that the methods used take account of the increase in
white-collar, professional, and business classes and the decrease
in the percentages of farmers, as well as other changes that
have occurred among American occupations from 1928 to
1952. We can now ask, Is there more or less opportunity than
formerly?

By using the same methods that were indicated for the previous calculations, we can allow 100 to stand for the perfect proportional representation between the percentages of men coming from the different occupations in 1928 and 1952. We shall
again present a table to summarize quickly what is known.
Table 5, "Who Got Their Share Yesterday and Today?" dis-

TABLE 5

WHO GOT THEIR SHARE YESTERDAY AND TODAY?

1928		1952	
	The Businessmen's Fathers Were:		
967	Businessmen	473	*Above*
433	Professional	350	*"Their Share"*
100 = Neither above nor below their share			
71	White-collar	80	*Below*
32	Farmers	33	*"Their*
24	Laborers	32	*Share"*

plays the ratios for businessmen for the two periods. Those occupations above the lateral line are proportionately above
their share, and those below are less than would be expected if
chance alone were operating. We shall start from the bottom
and move to the top, thus beginning with the laborers. In
1928, only 24 out of every 100 that might be expected were
sons of laborers, whereas in 1952 this figure rose to 32 out of
every 100. Among farmers the ratios remain practically identical for the two periods, but among white-collar men the
ratio moves from 71 to 80. Thus for the less highly ranked occupations there has been a decided increase in the proportion
of young men who have come from these more modestly placed
occupations in American society. When one inspects the ratios
for the two highly placed positions—businessmen and the professions—the exact reverse of what occurred in the other occupations is found to be true. For every 100 businessmen that
would have been expected, there were 967 in 1928, whereas in
1952 this had dropped to 473. Moreover, the sons of professional men dropped from 433 down to 350. Internal evidence
seems to indicate that the sons of those in the higher occupations do not seem to have the same opportunity or the same
motivation to go into these occupations as they did a generation ago. On the other hand, it is perfectly clear that the
sons of those in the lower occupations more often rise than they
did previously.

This analysis of the two principal elites—government and
business—seems to indicate that there is a considerable amount
of mobility from the bottom to the top; it indicates, of course,
that the birth elites are still at an advantage. However, the
figures also demonstrate that there is more mobility now than
previously. A similar statement for government men, partly
based on assumption, can be made. It is based on examination
of the kinds of men who previously occupied these positions
and from inspections of nonquantifiable material.

We have now reached the point where we can say that, insofar as our two populations permit us to go, there is more
mobility now, except for farmers, from all lower levels than

previously. And (within the competence of these investiga-
tions) clearly the society is more flexible. There is more opportunity for the individuals in business; more men do come
from the bottom. Furthermore, fewer sons of the wealthy stay
at the top in business than formerly. There is more circula-
tion from the bottom to the top and more movement out of the
top than previously. The top statuses (in business) are more
open to competition, and the principles of birth, while important and of great significance, do not operate as much as
they once did. In brief, the basic values of our society, including that nebulous but all-important belief in the American
dream, are more real now and less the stuff of legend and
fiction than they were a generation ago. Although we do not
have the quantitative evidence for the government leaders of
a generation ago, one must hypothecate from available evidence that, in all probability, there is also more mobility and
more opportunity in government than previously. The evidence
is strongly suggestive that other occupational hierarchies, including some of the professions, are more open than two generations before ours.

THE WOMEN THEY MARRY

Questions must now be asked: Why is this so? What is responsible for this condition, and how is mobility made possible for those born to less highly regarded occupational positions? We must first examine another important part of this
problem. The study of occupational succession is usually con-
fined to a comparison of the positions that men previously had
with those they occupy at the present time or to a generational
analysis of fathers and sons. While these studies are of the utmost importance and necessary, they do not tell us the full
story about the openness of a society and the freedom of movement from generation to generation. Particularly, they usually
leave out one half of the total population, namely, women and
wives. The principal mainstay of any inflexible closed caste
system is the control of marriage, the prevention of marriage
outside the caste—in brief, endogamy. In any open system of

rank the informal rules and the beliefs and values about marriage are such that there is marriage not only at the level of the men marrying but above and below; the marital rules are bimodal. The problem in this society is how much marriage is there at the level of big-business leaders and of the government executives. Do their sons marry at their own levels, or do they marry outside and below? If they marry women only at their own levels, we are indeed approaching a castelike society, even though there is considerable job mobility. If they

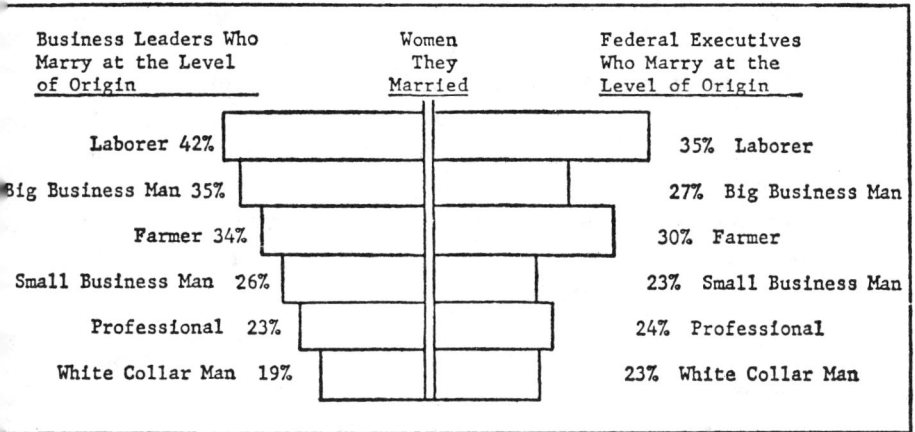

Business Leaders Who Marry at the Level of Origin	Women They Married	Federal Executives Who Marry at the Level of Origin
Laborer 42%		35% Laborer
Big Business Man 35%		27% Big Business Man
Farmer 34%		30% Farmer
Small Business Man 26%		23% Small Business Man
Professional 23%		24% Professional
White Collar Man 19%		23% White Collar Man

FIG. 1.   The wives of the business and government executives

marry in sufficient proportions outside and below themselves, the indications are strong that the society is far more fluid and open than it is rigid and closed.

Figure 1, "The Wives of the Business and Government Executives," tells much of what we need to know about the attitudes, behavior, and marriage of government and business leaders. Let us briefly indicate what the chart itself means. It will be noticed that at the top left-hand corner one reads "Business Leaders Who Marry at the Level of Origin," meaning their own origin, and at the right is a similar label for federal executives. Between the two is the label "Women They Married." The chart is laid out so that it gives quick understanding of the comparative proportions between the two; it tells what proportions of the executives in each of these two hierarchies of any particular origin marry at their own level. The story is rather eloquent. Of the businessmen who came from laboring origins, 42 per cent married at their own level; 35 per cent of those born to fathers who were big businessmen married women of their own class; some 34 per cent of those whose fathers were farmers married women whose fathers were farmers. The proportions drop down until the white-collar class is reached, where only 19 per cent of the men who were sons of clerks and salesmen married at the level at which they were born. In sum, these figures indicate that the two extremes of the occupational ranks are more likely to marry at their own level of origin. The farmers tend to greater isolation in their marriages as in their mobility; they tend to marry more frequently in their own class than do most other occupational levels and are not conspicuously mobile. These figures also indicate that the white-collar people are most likely to marry on and beyond the level of origin. Space does not permit us to analyze this material here, but tables available show that they marry at all class levels in larger proportions than do men from the other occupations.

A very similar story is told about the marriages of the government leaders. They too tend to marry more outside their level of origin than inside. But the principal difference between the government leaders and the business executives is that they are less likely to marry at their own level than businessmen. For example, 35 per cent of the men whose fathers were laborers married women of that class, whereas 42 per cent of the businessmen did. Only 27 per cent of the men whose fathers were big-business executives married at that level. The government men whose fathers were farmers married daughters of farmers in slightly smaller percentages than did the businessmen. The same is true for those whose fathers were small-business owners, but this is less true for those in the white-collar class. The only exceptions are the fathers who were in the professional and white-collar groups, where the percentages of marriage at their own level for the professions are about the same. The differences in most cases between the two elites are not very great. However, the marriages of the federal executives tend to be more exogamic than endogamic; they tend, insofar as the number of marriages are concerned, to be more open and flexible and less controlled by the values of status and rank than do those of the businessmen. In both cases, marriage is a product of feelings of rank and status strongly tempered by those of equalitarianism. Many of these figures show that, while many men marry at their own level, many more marry out; and, of those that marry out, some marry above themselves and some below.

Further examination of the details of these marriages show that all categories of occupational origin married into all other levels. However, when the men did marry "out," the farther away the occupations were from their own rank, the smaller the percentage of marriages; and the closer the occupational levels to their own, the greater the proportion of marriages among them.

As a general indicator of how the executives who were sons of laborers married beyond their own levels, it can be said that about the same percentage married the daughters of farmers as they did the owners of small business and white-collar men; a much smaller proportion married the daughters of professional men and big-business leaders. An opposite story is indicated by the marriages at the other extreme, the executives who were the sons of big-business leaders (it will be remembered 65 per cent married outside their own level): the largest number married the daughters of professional men and the owners of small business; a somewhat smaller percentage married the daughters of white-collar men; and a still smaller percentage married daughters of farmers and laborers.

In sum, the marriages of these two elites show that strong equalitarian principles are operating sufficiently to prevent closure and rigidity in the family system—that powerful system which governs much of the emotional behavior of the members of any society.

HIGHER EDUCATION AND THE MOBILITY OF GOVERNMENT AND BUSINESS EXECUTIVES

Since we know that there is a significant amount of movement from the bottom and the intermediate occupational levels up to the top levels of big business and big government, these questions once more present themselves: How do these men rise from the lower levels? What equipment do they have? And what are the factors involved that have helped increase mobility in this generation over the previous one? As everyone knows, more and more businessmen equip themselves with college and university training. During the course of this section of our discussion, we shall address ourselves to the basic question of the relation of education to career advancement of big businessmen. We shall first discuss the amount of education obtained by American business leaders and federal executives. We shall briefly indicate the kinds of colleges and give the names of those which trained many of these men. We shall answer these questions: How much education do the business and government leaders get? How many go to college? How many of them come up the hard way, stopping at elementary or high-school grade levels and going to work, to rise by the Horatio Alger route to success? Do the sons of business leaders get the same education as the executives who rise from the working class?

Let us examine how much education the business leaders and government executives obtain during their period of preparation for their careers. Table 6, called "Education: Who Gets It and How Much?" succinctly tells the story. The table is divided into two parts. On the left are the levels of education running from less than high school through to college graduation. Next are two columns of percentages, one giving the percentage of the adult male population who had reached a particular level and the second giving the percentage of business leaders who have that amount of education. To the right are the figures for 1959 (when the federal executive study was done)—the percentage of the U.S. male population of that time who had attained a particular educational level and the percentages of civilian federal executives. Thus comparisons can be made reliably among the several populations. Let us examine the business population first. It will be noted that 57 per cent of all the businessmen had graduated from college, well over half, and that some 19 per cent, another fifth, had gone to college for at least part of the four-year course. In brief, three fourths of all these men had had some college experience, whereas only 13 per cent of the adult males of the

TABLE 6

ᴇᴅᴜᴄᴀᴛɪᴏɴ: Wʜᴏ Gᴇᴛs Iᴛ ᴀɴᴅ Hᴏw Mᴜᴄʜ?

	1952		1959	
Education	*U.S. Adult Males (Per Cent)*	*Business Leaders (Per Cent)*	*U.S. Adult Males (Per Cent)*	*Civilian Federal Executives (Per Cent)*
Less than high school. 55		4	46	0
Some high school. 16		9	17	1
High-school graduation. 16		11	21	4
Some college. 6		19	7	14
College graduation. 7		57	9	81

United States had this amount of higher education. At the other extreme, 55 per cent of the adult male populations in 1952 had less than high school, whereas but 4 per cent of the businessmen had stopped at this lower level of attainment. The college graduation of businessmen was about eight times more than that of the general population. It might be added that about a third of these men went on to graduate study. All in all, these figures indicate that the contemporary businessman who occupies very high position (this at a mean age of fifty-four years) tends to be a highly educated man. There are clear indications of the rapid professionalization of this occupation, both by educational attainment and training and through later experience in business.

The statistics for higher education of top government executives are even more extreme. Less than one half of 1 per cent had less than high-school education, whereas 46 per cent of the U.S. adult male population in 1959 belonged in this category. On the other hand, 81 per cent, or more than eight out of ten of these men, had graduated from college, compared with 9 per cent of the U.S. male population. Fourteen per cent had some college, the combined totals reaching the rather astonishing figures of 95 per cent, or more than nine out of ten with college experience. Only 5 per cent had stopped after graduation from high school or with only some high-school experience. These executives are clearly highly educated; time does not permit us to go into the number of M.A.'s, Ph.D.'s, law, and other higher degrees among them, but the proportions are great and highly significant. There obviously is a built-in system of selection operating so that educational attainment is of the utmost importance in contributing to the careers of men in government and to their success in reaching top positions.

Although there has been a general increase in educational attainment in the total population in the country, there has been a still greater increase among business leaders. All groups, those born to each occupational class, show a higher percentage of university graduates today than did the sons of business leaders who were sons of the elite in the 1928 study of Taussig and Joslyn. This, of course, is an astonishing change, for today the sons of men who were workers get more education than those executives a generation ago who were the sons of big-business leaders.

Given the enormous importance of higher education as the principal route to success and as the principal source of attaining the skills necessary for doing the jobs at the top positions in government and business, we must ask, What kinds of university education did they get? What kinds of universities did they attend? For the businessmen, the Ivy League and private schools were the principal sources of educated men, but every variety of university of high or low esteem, sectarian or public school, contributed appreciably to the production of these men. However, one can ask, Did these men who come from other occupational levels attend the same types of universities as those who were born to the business elite and the professions? We shall give only summary answers. At the major Ivy League colleges very few sons of laborers were present. For example, although 16 per cent of the college graduates went to Harvard, Yale, or Princeton, all the fathers of the leaders who went to Harvard were either big-business or professional men. The same is true of Princeton and to a somewhat lesser degree, although not to the same categorical degree, of Yale. The Ivy League colleges, at the time these men were getting their education, tended to produce men who were born to top position. Since such a high proportion of all business leaders was educated, we need to ask Where did the executives who come from the lesser levels go to college? They attended large city and state universities, small sectarian colleges, and many went to technical schools such as M.I.T., Carnegie, and a few to the California Institute of Technology. Their undergraduate work tended to be in the liberal arts and the sciences and graduate training in business administration and law.

The colleges and universities from which the government executives received their higher training are different. We list in rank order the ten most popular institutions of higher learning for business and government in Table 7. It will be noted that several of the colleges where these men received their degrees are located in Washington, D.C., meaning that many received their college education while they were working in government service. Some of them are George Washington, Georgetown, and American University. It will also be noted that a few Ivy League schools, and only one in the strict sense of that term, produced graduates sufficiently to be in the first ten. Perhaps one of the most notable comments on the statistics of the first ten is the number of men who graduated from large state universities, including Minnesota, Wisconsin, California, Ohio State, and Michigan.

We can pursue our inquiry further by asking, Why is university education becoming the principal route to top executive position? Is it principally because of an advantage gained by use of academic training, resulting in an increase in competence? Or is a college degree merely an advantageous symbol of superiority that acts categorically so that the one who possesses it receives preferential treatment? Do the larger extracurricular experiences of university life, those over and

TABLE 7

THE TOP TEN UNIVERSITIES OF GOVERNMENT AND BUSINESS

Business	No.	Government	No.
Yale	1	George Washington	1
Harvard	2	Harvard	2
Princeton	3	Columbia	3
Cornell	4	University of Chicago	4
University of Pennsylvania	5	University of Minnesota	5
University of Illinois	6	Georgetown	6
Massachusetts Institute of Technology	6	University of Wisconsin	7
University of Michigan	6	University of California (Berkeley)	7
New York University	7	Ohio State	8
University of Minnesota	8	American University	8
Williams College	9	University of Michigan	9
University of California (Berkeley)	8	New York University	10
University of Chicago	10		

beyond the classroom, play the principal part in the leader's success? In brief, what factors are involved in the obvious success of the university men?[4]

In terms of career pattern, a number of generalizations can be made about college men. They tend to be promoted faster than noncollege men. The college-educated executives reach top positions at an earlier age than do the noncollege men. Most noncollege men obtain more education before they are promoted, indicating the need of education to support their

[4] The results of Dr. Robert Scofield's study, which was a continuation of the one on the big-business leaders, are used here. He examined the policy of promotion and inquired into the values and beliefs involved in the recruitment of college men by big-business organizations. The organizations included were selected from those Warner and Abegglen studied.

efforts for advancement. Moreover, noncollege men ordinarily serve a longer apprenticeship on the job before they are given the same occupational approval as the college man who possesses a degree when he arrives. During the earlier years of the college man's experiences in big business, the college degree does have some symbolic significance. Moreover, it permits better interpersonal relations and social intercourse with the superiors at a level that gives them greater equality with their superiors. However, the final choice for top positions is clearly not dependent on college degrees. At the time when a man reaches the position where he is promoted to the level at which we found him, the question of whether he has or has not a college degree is of little importance. What does matter is how well he performs on the job and the scope of his problem solving, his familiarity with the field, and his behavior as evaluated by the executive standards. It is significant that men who are born to high social status find a college degree important, and some of them necessary; a man who is born to high status often has more questions asked about why he did not get a college degree than one coming from lower occupational background.

The relationship of higher education to career achievement is important, but clearly other factors are operating to increase the use of higher education in business and government.

Why does education—university education—become such an important route to the top? Part of the answer is the massive changes that have occurred in the society which now favor the kind of training that takes place in college; and they are partly due to changes in the structure of business enterprise. There has been a change in the values and beliefs about what kinds of men are best fitted for advancement and what kinds of men are selected in the first place for employment and for future executive positions. The emphasis now tends to be more on the broadly trained man, who, it is believed, can make better decisions in a fluid and emergent society. There has been a change in management ideology about what it is that men should do at the top. Perhaps most important is the increase in size in many

of the industrial empires. A large number of them have grown
enormously. These are the companies which compete most
arduously in the recruitment of college men at their time of
graduation or after they have attended schools of business or
law or some other institution of advanced education. We
can only summarize what is demonstrably true from the research on big-business leaders.

When the big-business organizations were recategorized according to size, running from the very largest down to the
smaller ones, we were able to divide them into five levels. The
executives of each of these levels were then examined to determine what proportion of them had risen from lower to higher
occupational levels. An interesting generalization resulted from
this inquiry. The larger the business enterprise, the higher the
proportion of men who come from lower levels; the smaller
the size of the business enterprise, the smaller the proportion
of men from lower levels and the greater proportion born to
high position. It seems probable that if our inquiry had taken
us to still smaller enterprises—those which would be large, let
us say, for smaller cities and towns—the proportions of men
born to high position would have increased rather than decreased. In brief, mobility in business for the present day is
partly a function of the increasing complexity and the developing hierarchies of large enterprises. Moreover, it seems
probable that the educated man is more likely to be equipped
to make the decisions necessary in a society that is becoming
increasingly complex and be able to deal with the problems
that confront executives in high positions who must relate
their enterprises successfully to a rapidly changing world.
Higher education, which gives a broader view of the world
around the person so trained, fits closely with the needs and the
broad scope of large business enterprise. As such, it is also the
instrument by which the ambitious born to low position can
equip themselves to compete for top positions in government and business. It should be added that success breeds
success for higher education; for, with an increasing belief
and reliance on the ideology of those who select executives for

advancement, education is, if not a necessary requirement, then an increasingly advantageous characteristic for candidates for promotion.

We conclude our discussion of the specific problem of occupational mobility in American business and government with a brief comment on the larger problem of interpreting the significance of the results of the two researches in terms of the nature of the present society and in light of some of the contemporary and historical processes. The American society is a fluid, emergent one, with change in the nature of the system. The local communities merge into the larger national collectivity. Large-scale organizations, big government and big business, become increasingly prominent. In this fluid world of change and increasing immensity the managerial group will be drawn increasingly from the educated mobile men who come from the more populous lower occupational levels.

4

APPLYING BEHAVIORAL SCIENCE RESEARCH TO MANAGEMENT PROBLEMS

William Foote Whyte

THERE IS a process involved in applying behavioral science research to management problems. Unless research men and administrators understand the process, very little research will be applied. Here I shall attempt to cast some light on this process.

WHAT KIND OF RESEARCH?

First, let me ask what kind of behavioral science research business wants. We hear much discussion of basic versus applied research. This seems to me a false dichotomy. I would rather divide the general area of research into three categories.

One I would call "service research" or "information gathering." This might involve a morale questionnaire, for example, in which the researcher comes in, gathers information, passes it on to management, and then leaves for the next survey. It is as if the football coach did not have the opportunity to observe the game that his team was playing but occasionally had the score reported to him. At first, management people may be fascinated with all the nice data they are getting, but soon disillusion sets in. People come to want more than the scores. They want to know what plays went into making up the re-

125

ported scores and what plays to call for, in order to make better scores in the future. None of this information is provided in this sort of service research and information gathering.

Another type is commonly called "basic research." The researchers are studying fundamental scientific problems with no thought as to practical applications. There are one or two companies right now that are pushing behavioral science research in this way, and you would expect the first reaction of the behavioral scientist to this development to be one of enthusiasm. Here are companies with the vision to see that basic work in the behavioral sciences is worth supporting, and they are not pushing us for immediate application. However, I am inclined to think that this approach leaves much to be desired for business. In the first place, it is a possibility for only a few of the very largest companies with sufficient resources at their command that they can set aside a hundred thousand dollars or so to get a small group started and then have faith that sometime later it will pay off. Furthermore, I suspect this approach really retreats from reality rather than faces the problem of developing behavioral science research in a business setting. This is not the way that research becomes established in the business organization, if we can judge from the history of research in the natural sciences.

I have not studied this field, but I recall very well a conversation I had a few years ago with Dr. Eugene C. Sullivan, who, in the early years of the twentieth century, set up in the Corning Glass Works one of the first industrial research departments in this country. When he went to work without previous industrial experience, the practical operating people were dubious of his usefulness. He began on the problem of the signal lanterns on railroads which were manufactured by Corning Glass Works. They were having a great deal of trouble with cracked glass because of the heat inside and the extremes of temperature outside. Dr. Sullivan carried out some experiments and eventually developed railroad lantern glass that did not crack. This, you might say, was the birth of the research department at Corning Glass Works. After that it was not necessary to try to convince practical people that research had a role to play.

If behavioral science research is to be established in business, it has to be established on the basis of some proved payoff. Nor do I think that this undermines our scientific ideals, for I would like to advocate a third type of research that is both basic *and* applied. If this seems like a contradiction in terms, let me quote a statement by Chester I. Barnard[1] as he criticizes a report of the National Science Foundation which uses this dichotomy between basic and applied research:

> As one example, we have Karl Jansky's discovery of radio signals from outer space. Jansky, according to the report, was not engaged in basic research; he merely made a basic discovery. Here the confusion arises from labeling research according to the motives for which it is carried on; there is an element of snobbery involved which ought not to be encouraged. After all, Louis Pasteur made his great contributions to the foundations of bacteriology in trying to find solutions to the practical problems of the French silk and wine industries. The whole discussion demonstrates that the dichotomy between basic and applied research can be overemphasized.

Applying Barnard's idea to our own field, I would argue that research focused on a practical problem can also be basic research if it attempts to answer some general questions regarding the nature of human relations or the nature of organizational behavior.

THE APPLICATION PROCESS

Let us proceed to examine the application process. I should like to emphasize the word *process*, because I think one of the ways in which we have gone wrong in the past regarding application of research findings is that we have tended to assume, without thinking it through, that there was but a single jump from an invention to an application. The research man got the idea, checked it out through research, presented the idea, and people in the organization put it into practice.

---

[1] *Scientific American*, November, 1957.

This does not happen in human relations. Furthermore, it does not happen in engineering and the natural sciences either. In industry, we note that organizations set up research and development departments. Note the linking of the two. The process flow from research to invention (the discovery of an idea), to the development and testing of that idea, to pilot operation, and finally into production. This requires certain regularities in the interactions and activities of people. There is a work flow that goes through research and development departments. We not only observe it between the research and development people and operating management but also find it within research and development. For example, Ronken and Lawrence[2] trace the introduction of a new product in an electronics company where the usual flow goes from development engineers to industrial engineers and into production. In this case, the people who were actually researching and developing the idea were the industrial engineers, and the development engineers came in only at a later point. This reversal of the habitual pattern led to the conflicts and inefficiencies that the authors have so well described.

It is also important to note that research and development should be a continuing process. If there is a need for regularities to be developed in terms of interpersonal interactions and activities, this obviously cannot be done on the basis of a single invention which is then carried into application. Modern industrial organizations are constantly processing ideas. In this processing they develop the regularities on which efficiency and effectiveness depend.

This same approach can be applied to human relations research. I shall illustrate with three cases.

One of the best-known examples is the work done at Detroit Edison by the Survey Research Center at the University of Michigan under the general direction of Floyd Mann.[3] This in-

---

[2] *Administering Changes* (Boston: Harvard Graduate School of Business Administration, 1952).

[3] Floyd Mann and Rensis Likert, "The Need for Research on the Communication of Research Results," *Human Organization*, Vol. XI, No. 4 (1952).

volved a questionnaire survey program relating worker attitudes and perceptions to managerial leadership practices.
Line as well as staff people were actively involved in planning the research before the questionnaire was carried out.
Furthermore, a feedback process was planned even before the
study was carried into the field. The University of Michigan research staff began the feedback by carrying on discussion meetings first with top management, reviewing and interpreting
the findings with them, and helping them to interpret for
themselves. Then, instead of the university people reporting
directly to the lower levels, they got the line management
people to carry on these discussion meetings down through
the organization. In some divisions these feedback discussions
went down to the lowest supervisory level. The people who had
to apply the knowledge were themselves discussing how the
findings should be interpreted. A research man sat in on
meetings as a resource person, to be called on for technical
points, but the responsible supervisor conducted the meeting
for his group.

Another example, and perhaps the most impressive of all, I
have come to think, is represented by Glacier Metals in Eng-
land. It began in about 1944 through collaboration with the
Tavistock Institute of Human Relations and the Glacier company. For the company, the key man was Wilfred Brown, managing director. The chief man involved for Tavistock was
Elliott Jaques, a psychiatrist and a very gifted behavioral scientist. The research program first focused on consultative processes. The company had works councils, so that there was
active consultation with workers and with union leaders, and
there was also a pattern of management meetings. Management in general and Mr. Brown in particular felt that the company's efforts were fumbling in this respect. Management
did not know just exactly what it was doing. In order to develop a better understanding of the human processes that
were going on, Jaques served as an observer in these meetings.
From time to time he discussed with the council representa-
tives, union officers, and management officials what he thought

he saw taking place and helped them in this way to conceptualize the human processes involved in these organizational relationships. The first major part of this effort appeared in a book some years ago, *The Changing Culture of a Factory* by Jaques.[4]

Then Jaques changed his relationship somewhat. He became employed directly by the company but still functioned in quite an independent fashion. Now he began to work on problems involving what we would call wage and salary administration and job evaluation. The discussion process had previously revealed that there were constant problems coming up regarding supposed inequities in pay. How do you establish what will be accepted generally as the right level of pay for a given job? This also involves, of course, the relation of job A with job B and job C and so on. After a good deal of exploration of this area, Jaques developed a theory of the time span of responsibility—the notion that the main criterion by which people were implicitly evaluating the importance of a job involved the length of time after which the decisions the individual took were, in the normal course of events, subject to evaluation and review. Thus, at the very bottom level, what the individual did was frequently checked upon, whereas, at the higher-management levels, it might take five years or more before a decision taken by a given individual could be shown to have been a good decision or not. There were, of course, many gradations in between. This approach has been described in Jaques' book, *The Measurement of Responsibility*.[5]

I am not here concerned with evaluating the scientific merits of this theory. I am concerned with application, and here we have Managing Director Brown's report that this analytical approach has been applied in the company to wage and salary administration and to job evaluation. Brown also states that this approach has resulted in a much more equitable system of pay and much more general satisfaction with the pay system.

Finally, there has appeared what I think is a rather extraordi-

[4] London: Tavistock Publications, Ltd., 1951.

[5] London: Tavistock Publications, Ltd., 1956.

nary book by the managing director himself—*Exploration in Management*.⁶ It seems to me that Wilfred Brown's book ranks with Chester Barnard's classic, *Functions of the Executive*,⁷ as one of the few books written by management people that add significantly to our understanding of organizations and organizational processes. Brown freely acknowledges that his own thinking has been shaped in a major way by the research carried on by Jaques and by the constant consultation between them. I am sure that this has not been one-sided. Jaques has been immensely stimulated by these discussions with Brown.

I cannot undertake to sum up all that has come out in the Brown book, but let me state what seems to me the basic idea underlying the detailed conclusions. Brown points out that in many cases in his organization there have been serious discrepancies between the behavior that actually went on and management's conceptions of what was going on. It was Brown's theory that if you examine these discrepancies, if you become more aware of what is going on and re-examine your own beliefs about how the organization functions, you will make progress in one of two directions. You will change your behavior to bring it into line with your growing understanding of organizational processes, or you will change your theories of organization to bring them into line with behavior—or you will do some of both. Whatever adjustments are made, a major product is increased conceptual clarity. The idea is that you can act more effectively as a manager to the extent that you have a reasonably accurate and systematic understanding of what it is you are doing and how the organization is functioning. While specific research applications could be noted, the really major accomplishment was the development of a new framework of organizational theory—and the changes in organizational structure and processes implied in that theory.

My third case is not generally known, but I hope to make it

---

⁶ New York: John Wiley & Sons, Inc., 1960.
⁷ Cambridge: Harvard University Press, 1938.

more known by means of writing a book about it.[8] This involves an action research program that I was involved in some years ago with Meredith Wiley and Edith Lentz. In 1945 the Tremont Hotel (as we call it) was beset by very difficult personnel problems, high turnover, interpersonal frictions, and general disorganization. The top executive, who took a sudden interest in our research approach, invited me to recommend to him a new personnel manager. Upon learning that there had been three men on that job in the previous year, I came to the conclusion that it was a hazardous position, to which I would not want to recommend any friend of mine or any student. I proposed a different approach: that if the top executive (Mr. Smith, let us call him) was really serious regarding a new approach to personnel administration, I would recommend to him a man I thought could do a good job as personnel manager. I would also send him a field research worker, who would study the human problems of the organization. I would direct the research side of it and consult with the personnel manager and with Mr. Smith and others in management. That was our agreement.

Meredith Wiley, a student of ours at the University of Chicago, went on the payroll as personnel manager. Edith Lentz, who had worked with me in the restaurant industry study, carried on the field research. The research notes came to me and to Mr. Wiley and to no one else in the organization, although a number of people expressed curiosity about them.

We set to work, trying first to discover what the human problems were and then to feed our findings into the organization through Personnel Manager Wiley in such a fashion that the problems would be relieved. The process in the individual departments went something like this. Mr. Wiley and Miss Lentz would consult with the responsible management in the department about the nature of the problems and about arrangements that could be made regarding the interviewing and observation. Miss Lentz would then move in on the department, observing the work as it proceeded and interviewing

---

[8] *Action Research for Management,* in process.

the employees, either on or off the job. We gave in advance commitments about confidentiality. We would not reveal who said what but would give our feedback in general terms—and first at the department head level, not at the top. Nor did we try to present the findings all digested and analyzed. Our aim was to present the data and help the department head to make his own analysis of the problems.

Let me give a few examples of the kinds of changes we were able to bring about. I pick these examples not necessarily because they were the most important but because they indicate the range of our concern. We were concerned, for example, at one point with a change in technology. This may seem a dignified term for changing the location of a water spigot in a restaurant, but this was a vital problem at the time for the girls in a very busy coffee shop who had to walk outside the room altogether—some hundred-odd feet—every time they wanted to get water for the customers. They had been put off on this by the story that the whole hotel was going to be renovated and there would be new water spigots everywhere in the future, so they should not bother management with such complaints. Now this had become a symbol of management's lack of concern for the welfare of the employees. "They won't give us a water spigot, so what do they care about us?" Wiley had to take the problem up to the highest level—and we got the water spigot.

Work flow is generally thought of as in the province of the industrial engineer, but we got into a work-flow problem with the checkers. At the end of the kitchen where the waiters and waitresses went through to the three dining rooms, there was one checker stand with three checkers. Lines of waiters and waitresses converged at this point and went out in three different directions. Each checker had a combination accounting and supervisory responsibility. She totaled checks, but she also told the waitresses and waiters when they did not have the proper things on the tray, and she could send them back to the kitchen. So that the checkers would have enough to do, they also handled the room-service telephone. It took just a little observation of the work flow, of the traffic problems, and of the rise of the interpersonal temperatures as the rush hour got under way to indicate the necessity of some drastic changes. On the basis of Miss Lentz's report, Mr. Wiley worked out with the hotel engineer and the supervisors in question the establishment of a second checker stand and the rerouting of the traffic so as to relieve congestion and reduce tensions.

A problem of organization structure confronted us in the housekeeping department, where a manager had been superimposed upon a woman who had previously been in charge of the department. The two were constantly at sword's points. After observing this battle going on and the frictions and confusions that arose at the lower levels, we worked out, in consultation with them, a change in organizational structure. In effect, we divided the house into two parts. The manager, retaining over-all responsibility, assumed charge of the public rooms, and his assistant took charge of the guest rooms. With this (and other) changes, the friction subsided.

Perhaps our major effort involved a rechanneling of communication patterns. We found tremendous pressures coming down from the top. This was autocratic supervision in extreme form, with Mr. Kraus, the resident manager (the No. 2 man) having, as his main approach to personnel, the periodic reading of the riot act, as he himself called it. It was his theory that this would keep people on their toes.

In certain departments where we did research, we stimulated a series of group meetings whereby the supervisor would lead discussions with the employees of the problems they faced and encourage them to make suggestions for changes. In order to establish effective group meetings, we had to provide some insulation from the top levels. One of my early efforts in leading a top-management meeting involved a report ostensibly from our restaurant industry study. I discussed the baleful effects on nervous tension and efficiency at the lower levels of unrelieved downward pressure. My remarks were enthusiastically endorsed by Mr. Smith—who was a great source of pressure himself. This had the effect of restraining Mr. Kraus, the No. 2 man, so that he discontinued his reading of riot acts. As these departmental meetings began to bring results, so that the tension was reduced and the employees themselves were giving testimonials about the improved work atmosphere and Mr. Smith was even claiming to notice greater efficiency in the operation, we began to get group meetings established as a regular pattern.

Not only did we promote the idea of holding group meetings, we also provided feedback to the people holding the meetings. For example, after the first series of meetings in the Housekeeping Department, Miss Lentz carried on interviews with a number of maids and found them appreciative but still saying that certain things that the manager and assistant manager said in the meetings would embarrass them and make them feel as if they were on the spot, so that they could not talk as freely as they wished. They could not say this directly to the manager, but they could say it to Miss Lentz. She and Mr. Wiley were then able to discuss the criticisms in general with the executives. Thereafter, we noted the elimination of the behavior that had been dampening the freedom of expression in meetings. Though he conducted no formal courses, Mr. Wiley was doing leadership training all the time—training based on research findings.

One of the secrets of whatever we accomplished was the manner in which we were able to provide rewards indirectly for the supervisors from the lowest levels on up. As I have noted, we did not report at the top level or at any high level first. Anything we reported at the top level was of a very general nature, something like "We're working on it, and we will let you know later." When we did report on problems to higher levels, it was in terms of what the given supervisor had been able to accomplish in improvement in his own department. This brought the supervisor recognition from higher management, and it also tended to establish a new set of symbols. In effect, we were managing to change what behavior was rewarded, although we did not give the reward directly.

What came out of it? I do not want to dwell at length on the results because they were largely things that we could not precisely measure. One measure we did have. When we started, turnover stood at almost 25 per cent a month. Eighteen months later, it was down to between 4 and 6 per cent a month. Unfortunately, we do not have comparable figures from other hotels in the same city because records were not kept at the time. On the marked changes in human relations, we had ample—if not readily quantifiable—data.

INSIDE OR OUTSIDE?

I have given certain examples of the application of research findings. Now I should like to face the question "Where should this sort of research be fitted into the organization?"

There are three main possibilities. It can be all inside, that is, all carried on by employees of the company. It can be all outside, carried on by people at universities or by consulting firms. Or it can be mixed, a combination of the two.

It seems to me that the all-inside arrangement presents some serious problems. There is a status problem in communicating. Your active research people will be a number of notches in status below the level of the management people whose behavior they need to influence which makes for some difficulties in getting a response. Then there is the question of whether publication is encouraged or stifled. Can you go beyond just reporting the data back to the organization? If not, you will not be able to recruit and retain good research people.

Recently I was talking with a very able young research man who I thought was developing a very effective research program within his company. Not thinking that we could attract him, I asked him if he might possibly have any interest in a teaching and research job that we had to offer. He said, "Two months ago, I would have said no. But now, let me think about it. I have to take this up at higher levels because, while they have been very happy about my research and with the feedback I have given them, there are all sorts of further analyses that I want to make with these data—things that I want to write up for publication. I am not sure that the company is at all interested in this. They seem to want me to start the next study right away."[9]

There is also a problem of instability. I have seen company research units started with high promise. They go up and down in response to the business cycle. In management thinking, this activity is apparently expendable. But when a company gets the reputation for taking in good people and then dropping them when times get a little tight, it becomes harder to recruit good people in the future. Then there have been all sorts of problems of organization and reorganization, so that some companies seem to have spent more time in placing and replacing their research people than they have in actually getting the job done.

The all-outside solution has the advantage of status freedom. If I do research within a company, I can communicate with people at any level from worker up to chairman of the board— and have, on occasion. But there are serious drawbacks. There is a good deal of knowledge of organizational politics that the outsider lacks. He could learn it, but if he takes all his time to learn it, he will not get on with his research job. It is very helpful to have some sort of official guides to the politics of the organization working with you. Finally, the all-outside solution tends to lack continuity and follow-through. It tends to be a short-time proposition, although there are exceptions to this rule.

The mixed solution seems to me perhaps the ideal to aim at. But a number of combinations are possible here. The idea of having occasional consultation from a behavioral scientist does not seem to me very profitable. It may be financially profitable to the behavioral scientist, but I seriously doubt the value of such advice tossed off by any of us, myself included. I think what we need to arrive at is some kind of working arrangement with people inside the organization who share some

---

[9] Fortunately, this does not seem an insoluble problem. Because of the understanding—and effective maneuvering—of the man in charge of personnel research activities, this research man was given 9 to 12 months of complete freedom from other responsibilities, so that he could devote himself entirely to further analysis and writing.

responsibility for the research. I have described three cases of this nature. Let me describe another possibility that may hold some interest.

I have recently become involved in a program of the Prudential Insurance Company. In their Planning and Research Department they set up what they call the President's Advisory Council on Research. To get it called the President's Council, they, of course, had to have it approved by the president and to get a commitment from him that he would be actively involved in it.

They picked five social scientists—two economists, William Baumol and J. K. Galbraith; political scientist Harold Lasswell; and two sociologists, Paul Lazersfeld and me. The idea was that we would sit down with them several times a year and canvass with them their ideas and ours of the research they might do and how they might go about it. Our advice was sought also on matters of policy. Finally, each of us was to be available to work most closely with that research unit of the company with which we shared the closest interest. The company indeed does have a wide range of research activities, all the way from economic analysis to organizational studies.

This kind of arrangement has certain advantages to social scientists. Money you might think of first, but I do not think this is very important. It may be a relief to Prudential policyholders to know that the money we receive is adequate but not lush. I am sure any of us could make equivalent money in other outside activities. The appeal is more in other lines. It involves working with a very stimulating group of researchers, company members as well as members of the council. It also involves developing a growing knowledge of an interesting organization through working with it over a period of time. Finally, it offers an opportunity to stimulate particular lines of research without having to carry the responsibility of getting the research job done itself.

What does Prudential get out of it? Obviously, I am not the best one to tell, but I have certain notions that may perhaps be accurate. This device of setting up a council whose meetings will be attended at least part of the time by such people as the president of the company, the executive vice-presidents, and the department heads serves to give the activity status. It focuses top-level attention on research. Also I am confident that it enables us to give the company much better advice regarding research than any of us could provide if we were called in only on a casual basis. Together, we are gradually developing a good deal of background on their problems and on the way they operate in the insurance business and in research. Besides, we seem to stimulate each other when we get together.

The council also helps to establish priorities for research. Prudential has quite a long history of social research. Currently they have a number of projects going on and others under consideration. The company has neither the personnel nor the resources to pursue all the interesting project ideas. It may thus be very important to arrive at a judgment that Project A is more likely to provide useful knowledge than Project B.

Finally, the council may stimulate a better integration of the projects that management is carrying on. Given a degree of decentralization of research throughout the company, we have found that many of the things carried on in one department have relevance for another department. To some extent, management people have been aware of this, but our meetings have helped to elucidate these relationships and may perhaps have pointed the way to a more integrated research program.

LOCATION WITHIN COMPANY STRUCTURE

I have been discussing the inside-versus-outside location of this research unit without saying specifically where it might be located if it is inside. It might be located in a Research and Development Department. This perhaps has advantages in terms of locating behavioral science research with other scientific research. It also has the hazard that we may become the poor relation of the Research and Development organization. Much would depend on the vision and the interest of the top research administrator.

Perhaps the more natural location would seem to be within the Personnel Department, and yet the kind of thing that we are doing seems foreign to most such departments. In Personnel there seems to be a preoccupation with techniques and systems, records and programs, merit rating, job evaluation training, and so on. On the other hand, the personnel man is expected to be a consultant to line management on human relations problems. It is this responsibility that provides the need and the hope for the development of research within this organizational unit. How can the personnel manager be an effective consultant if he does not have any data to report that are not available to other people in the organization? The accountant, the engineer, the natural scientist, all have their esoteric data that they have a command over, far beyond the line people. But everybody will claim to be an expert on human relations, and the personnel man will not get very far if he just tries to match his hunches against those of other people. Only if he can report data that others do not have and analyze those data more effectively than others can, will he deserve the respect that should be accorded the role of consultant.

CONCLUSION

I have tried to show that application involves far more than the discovery of bits of knowledge. Application is a social process. Those who do it well will do so because they have learned to organize the flow of research activities and integrate that flow with the structure and processes of the management organization.

5

PSYCHOLOGICAL STUDIES OF RISKY DECISION MAKING[1]

R. Duncan Luce

INTRODUCTION

AT THE outset, let me acknowledge my ignorance of the world of business. Professionally, I have had little to do with business or with its study, and so I write with no more than an educated layman's understanding of which intellectual endeavors are relevant to business problems. Because of this, it would be foolish and presumptuous to claim that the studies we shall examine here are directly applicable to them. I suspect that my general problem—the choices that people make among alternatives whose consequences are risky—is of quite general interest; however, specific theories and experiments may very well be another matter. But even if what I describe is not of direct relevance to business, hopefully it will be at least intriguing. I plan simply to sketch some of the ideas and findings that theoretical and experimental psychologists have made in this stimulating, confusing, and conflictful area of research.

The problem is, let me repeat, to describe the formal struc-

[1] This is a slightly revised and retitled version of an address given in the School of Commerce, University of Wisconsin, April 11, 1961. The work was supported in part by grant NSF-8864 from the National Science Foundation to the University of Pennsylvania.

ture of a person's choices when the consequences following
from a choice are risky. That is, we are searching for a
satisfactory abstract—mathematical—description of a person
choosing among two or more alternatives, each of which is,
in more familiar terms, a lottery or gamble. Although the
specific outcome to him depends to some extent on his choice,
it also depends on chance events that are quite beyond his
control.

Some early mathematicians were interested in choices among
money gambles. It was Daniel Bernoulli, for example, who so
neatly established that people do not choose on the basis of
expected money returns alone. Out of these early studies grew,
on the one hand, the mathematical notions of probability and,
on the other hand, the economic notions of cardinal utility
for nonnumerical commodities. Although separately evolved,
these two groups of ideas have always had a close affinity, and
less than 15 years ago they were reunited in the work of von
Neumann and Morgenstern, Savage, and Wald, to name only
the most prominent contributors.

Even though history seems to suggest that our problem lies
in the province of economics and statistics, it is evident that in
part it also belongs to psychology. Indeed, I think the claim
can be defended that the study of the choices which individuals and institutions should make to attain certain ends
forms a part of—and quite possibly is equivalent to—statistics; that the study of the choices which individuals do in
fact make forms a part of—but definitely is not equivalent to—
psychology; and that the study of the choices which aggregates
of people and institutions make forms a part of economics and
sociology. That much theoretical work about the choices
that individuals make when the alternatives are risky appears
in the economic literature is, it seems to me, no more than a
historical accident. Some approaches to economics seem to demand psychological underpinnings, and economists have never
been loath to create their own psychologies when none could
be borrowed.

Accepting that the descriptive half of the problem of

individuals making choices belongs to psychology, what then have we done to solve it? Speaking broadly, there have been two mathematical tacks. One group of psychologists has developed models which, although different in detail, are similar in spirit to those proposed by the economists. These theories have been designed to account for the results of preference studies. For the most part, they have been applied only to choices among what we may call "sure" alternatives, i.e., to those for which the outcome depends only on the subject's choice and not on any other events. Usually, there is no reason why preference theories cannot be applied to risky alternatives, but, until recently, such theories have failed to include in their structure the added richness provided by dealing with risky alternatives.

A second group of psychologists concerned with the processes of human learning have, almost inadvertently, studied choices among risky alternatives. Their end was not to understand the interrelations among the choices that subjects make in different situations of risk but rather to use these situations as devices to generate particular temporal patterns of responses. The subjects in these experiments initially know little or nothing about the events controlling the outcomes that result from their choices. But the same choices are offered over and over, and, in the course of time, the subjects acquire considerable statistical information about the events. Ultimately, their responses settle down to some stable pattern of behavior, much like that discussed by the utility and preference theorists. During the past decade, a sizable mathematical literature has evolved in the attempt to describe this and related sorts of learning.

So, in total, we have three general classes of theories which attempt to describe an individual's choices among risky alternatives—the economists' and statisticians' utility theories and the psychologists' preference and learning theories. The distinction between utility and preference theory is often somewhat fuzzy, for to a considerable extent it rests upon who did the work. I shall sharpen it for present purposes by restricting attention to those utility theories centered around the expected utility hypothesis and to those preference theories explicitly assuming stochastic behavior.

SUBJECTIVE EXPECTED UTILITY THEORIES

A characteristic of all utility theories, expected or otherwise, is that one can assign numerical quantities—utilities—to alternatives in such a way that alternative *a* is chosen from a set *T* of alternatives if and only if the utility of *a* is larger than that of any other alternative in *T*. When such an assignment is possible, we say that the person behaves optimally relative to his utility scale, that he maximizes utility.

When we study risky alternatives, we have a second guiding idea which is called the "subjective expected utility hypothesis." It holds that, in addition to utility assignments to all alternatives—risky as well as sure—one can also assign numbers to events. The numbers are interpreted as the subject's evaluation of the likelihood of the event's occurring; they are called "subjective probabilities." Like ordinary objective ones, they lie between 0 and 1. These two numerical scales are interlocked in the following way: the utility of a risky alternative is the sum of the utilities of its component outcomes, each weighted according to the subjective probability of its occurring. For example, if $a\alpha b$ denotes the risky alternative in which *a* is the outcome when the event α occurs and *b* when it fails to occur, then the subjective expected utility hypothesis asserts in this simple case that

$$u(a\alpha b) = u(a)\psi(\alpha) + u(b)[1 - \psi(\alpha)],$$

where *u* denotes the utility scale and ψ the subjective probability scale.

The primary theoretical problem has been to justify this representation. Typically, a series of empirically testable assumptions is stated which relate choices one to another, and from these it is shown by mathematical argument that the expected utility representation follows. The assumptions made are always plausible as canons of rational behavior. For example, they usually include one something like this: when *a* is preferred to b and when event α is more likely than event β, then $a\alpha b$ is preferred to $a\beta b$. Usually it is easy to persuade oneself and one's more rational friends that one should abide by these axioms, but rather fewer of us are willing to claim that they actually describe our behavior.

There are three major theories of this type. In 1947 von Neumann and Morgenstern (35) stated the first such system of axioms, which served as a normative underpinning for their theory of games. As a normative theory it may well be satisfactory, but as description it was badly marred by the supposition that objective probability can substitute for subjective probability. In 1954, Savage (31) rectified this weakness by incorporating into a single, elegant axiom system both their utility ideas and de Finetti's (19, 20) subjective probability notions. Although this is probably the definitive axiomatization, other more special ones are often useful. For example, Davidson and Suppes (9), working out an idea suggested in 1931 by the philosopher Ramsey (30), developed a utility theory that required only data from choices among gambles generated by but one event—one having a subjective probability of ¼. This considerably simplifies certain experimental problems.

Only two major empirical studies have been carried out, one to test the von Neumann-Morgenstern theory and the other the Davidson-Suppes theory. Without directly examining the correctness of the von Neumann-Morgenstern axiom system, Mosteller and Nogee (29) applied the expected utility equation, using objective probabilities, to certain observed choices and attempted to construct individual utility functions for money. They found that such functions could, in fact, be calculated and that they were reasonably smooth, increasing functions of money. With these functions in hand and again assuming the expected utility hypothesis, they then predicted the subject's choices between risky alternatives different from those used to construct the functions. These predictions, although somewhat more accurate than those calculated from expected money returns, were far from perfectly accurate. By strict standards, the model failed, but the failure was ambiguous. Did it stem from the expected utility hypothesis itself or from the equating of subjective to objective probability? No one could be sure.

The second study, performed by Davidson, Suppes, and Siegel (10), required only an event having a subjective probability of ½. With that in hand, the utility function was generated by carrying out an extremely careful exploration of the choices made when the money outcomes were changed by 1-cent amounts. Although a 1-cent change is small in absolute value, it was actually a sizable percentage change of the sums involved: from 3 to 25 per cent. The most important consequence of this procedure was that it prevented an exact determination of the utility function; only upper and lower bounds could be found. Once the bounds were determined, the experimenters tested the theory in much the same way as Mosteller and Nogee by predicting choices in situations different from those used to generate the utility functions. Because of the indeterminacy of the utility functions, however, a number of the more sensitive predictions could not be made. Of those that were unambiguous, an extremely high proportion were correct.

It is generally agreed that this experiment provides the strongest support for the subjective expected utility hypothesis as a description of behavior, but, even so, its success is equivocal. One doubts that the hypothesis has been adequately taxed both because of the indeterminacy of the utility function and because the theory is restricted to only one chance event.

Several other experimental studies have been interpreted as unfavorable to the expected utility hypothesis (Coombs [6]; Coombs and Pruitt [7]; and Edwards [11–14, 16]). Some of these have been concerned with preferences among gambles having different money variances but the same expected values, and others with preferences among the probabilities of the events themselves. For example, Edwards' subjects chose between bets having the same expected money values. When that expectation was positive, they consistently preferred those bets with a 50:50 chance of winning and avoided those with a 75:25 chance; when the expected value was negative, these preferences were reversed.

It is not easy to know what to make of such studies. For one thing, the gambles all involve only two outcomes, and so when one variable, such as variance, is changed, others, such as range, must also automatically change. Thus it is impossible to know which of several variables is actually relevant to the behavior. For another, most, if not all, of the results are explicable in terms of the subjective expected utility hypothesis, provided that we are willing to accept utility and subjective probability functions with enough twists and bends.

Where do we stand? It is impossible at present to cite a study either clearly supporting or clearly rejecting the subjective expected utility hypothesis. Because of the freedom to select both the utility and the subjective probability functions, I do not find it surprising that we have been unable clearly to reject it. What would be truly surprising would be for the experimental evidence to fail to give strong support, were the hypothesis in fact correct. This, coupled with the peculiar results that Edwards and others have obtained, has made some psychologists suspicious that, at least in detail, the subjective expected utility hypothesis is wrong. A number of us suspect that the structure of choices is somewhat more subtle than can be satisfactorily encompassed by this very simple and appealing model. Of course, it may well turn out that under some conditions this model is a good approximation to a more nearly correct one, but we probably will not know what the conditions are until we have discovered the more correct one. Consequently, many of us have turned to other approaches.

PREFERENCE THEORIES

An incidental result of the Mosteller-Nogee experiment which has since been seen in a number of other studies is that subjects are not always consistent in their choices. If a pair of alternatives is presented many times, successive presentations being well separated by other choices, a given subject does not necessarily choose the same alternative each time. At first, one is tempted to attribute such inconsistency to changes of state in the subject or to other errors of measurement, much as one would in testing a physical theory. There are, however, two features of the data which lead one to suspect that the phenomenon may in fact be basic to the choice process. The pattern of inconsistency is very regular when it occurs. For

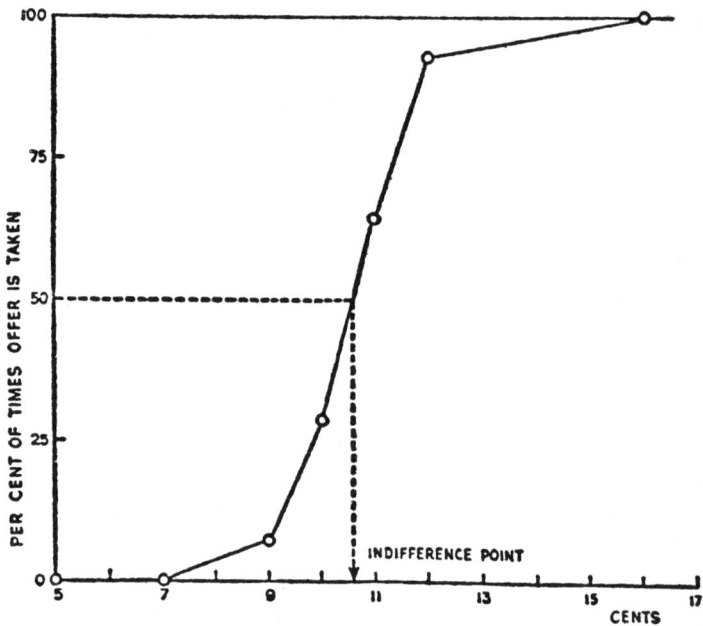

FIG. 1. Percentage of times a gamble of the form $x\alpha - 5\phi$, where event α has a probability 0.332 of occurring, was chosen over nothing as reported by Mosteller and Nogee (29, Fig. 2). This figure is reproduced with permission of the *Journal of Political Economy*.

example, suppose the two alternatives are the gamble $x\alpha - 5\phi$ and the pure outcome nothing. When x is small, say 1ϕ, the gamble is never chosen: when it is larger, say \$1, it is always chosen. And as x varies from 1ϕ to \$1, the probability of choosing the gamble increases in a smooth S-shaped curve, such as that shown in Figure 1. In contrast, there are other pairs, such as x versus nothing, where the behavior is perfectly discontinuous: when $x < 0$, x is never chosen, and when $x > 0$, it is always chosen. It appears that a wonderfully complex error theory will be needed to account for such different results. As an alternative to treating these results as errors, we can try to construct inherently probabilistic choice models. The postulates so far suggested are numerous and their interrelations complex; much of this net of implications was worked out by Block and Marschak (2) and by Marschak (28). Of the various postulates, the two that have received most empirical attention are weak and strong stochastic transitivity. In both it is assumed that we have three alternatives—a, b, and c—such that when a and b are presented, the subject selects a at least half the time and that when b and c are presented, he chooses b at least half the time. The question is what happens when a and c are presented. Weak stochastic transitivity says that a will be chosen at least half the time. Strong stochastic transitivity says that the proportion of times a is selected over c will be at least as large as the proportion of times a is selected over b and at least as large as the proportion of times b is selected over c. In symbols, if $P(a,b) \geqslant \frac{1}{2}$ and $P(b,c) \geqslant \frac{1}{2}$, then weak transitivity says simply that $P(a,c) \geqslant \frac{1}{2}$, and strong says that $P(a,c) \geqslant P(a,b)$ and $P(b,c)$. Strong clearly implies weak transitivity, and it reduces to ordinary algebraic transitivity when the probabilities are 0 or 1.

Neither assumption is strong enough to stand alone as a theory of behavior—certainly not as a theory about choices among risky alternatives, because nothing is assumed about the nature of the alternatives. Aside from a certain a priori reasonableness, they are of interest mainly because weak transitivity is a consequence of practically every more elaborate stochastic theory that has been proposed and strong transitivity, of many. Thus, should we collect data that rejected either, with it would be swept away many other proposed theories.

Almost any preference study that one might perform affords an opportunity to test these hypotheses, but few, if any, studies that have been performed provide, in my view, adequate tests. Davidson and Marschak (8) obtained single observations from each subject for each pair of alternatives in several triplets. Because single observations do not permit very subtle estimates of probabilities, they were forced to a subtle statistical analysis to test the two hypotheses. Although they interpret their results as supporting both, it would have required such extreme data to reject either that I do not find their evidence very convincing. Chipman (5) and Coombs and Pruitt (7) made several observations for each pair of alternatives, estimated the choice probabilities from these, and tested the two hypotheses. The authors in both cases concluded that strong transitivity may well be wrong. For example, Coombs and Pruitt found that strong transitivity was violated in 25 per cent of the triples where it could be tested. However, as they point out, one is bound to have some apparent rejections as a result of sampling variability, and when each probability is estimated from only 6 or 8 observations, as was the case in these two studies, one suspects that this may be quite a serious problem. No one has yet worked out the necessary statistical analysis to know whether their results should be accepted at face value. Griswold and Luce (22) employed 30 to 50 observations per pair to estimate the choice probabilities, and among 103 triples of money gambles they found a total of 13 violations of strong transitivity. Moreover, most of these violations were within one standard deviation of the quantities estimated and so may very well not really indicate violations. In their opinion, there was no substantial reason to doubt strong transitivity.

As I have said, neither transitivity assumption is a complete theory of behavior, and neither has anything in particular to do with risky alternatives; so let me consider next a theory which is restricted to that case. It is described in detail in *Individual Choice Behavior* (Luce [24]). The basic assumptions are three forms of statistical independence. The first, called the "choice axiom," is a probabilistic version of the ubiquitous independence of irrelevant alternatives notion in decision theory (Luce and Raiffa [26]). It says that the probability of choosing alternative *a* from a set *S* of alternatives is identical with the conditional probability of choosing *a* from a larger set *T*, provided that we consider only those choices which, in fact, lie in *S*, i.e.,

$$P_S(a) = P_T(a|S),$$

assuming that the conditional probability exists. For example, suppose that two thirds of the time a person selects steak over lamb chops when they are the only two alternatives. Suppose we now confront him with chicken and liver as well as steak and lamb chops, and let us look only at those occasions when he selects either steak or chops. The axiom asserts that the relative frequency of steak choices will be exactly the same as when the chicken and liver were not present, namely, two thirds.

Our second major assumption limits the theory to risky alternatives. Suppose one must choose between $a\alpha b$ and $a\beta b$. There are two conditions when one should prefer the former, namely, when one prefers *a* to *b* and judges α as more likely than β and also when one prefers *b* to *a* and judges β more likely than α. If we suppose that a person's preference decisions are statistically independent of his judgments of likelihood, then

$$P(a\alpha b,\ a\beta b) = P(a,b)Q(\alpha,\beta) + P(b,a)Q(\beta,\alpha),$$

where *P* denotes the preference probability and *Q* the judgment probability. This has been called the "decomposition axiom."

The third assumption is the choice axiom applied to likelihood selections among events; it is the same equation as before with *Q* replacing *P* and events replacing alternatives.

Of the two results I shall cite, the second leads to an experimental test of the theory. Recall that there are data which suggest that the probability paint is spread somewhat unevenly over the pairs of risky alternatives. The decomposition theory not only allows this to happen but in a sense requires it. Specifically, it can be shown either that the choice probabilities for pairs of sure alternatives are 0, ½, or 1, as happens with money, or that the probabilities of judging one event as more likely than another can assume only three possible values. The probabilities of choice among gambles are not so severely restricted. This somewhat surprising and strong result has, on the whole, made psychologists skeptical of the theory. There is a common view that weaker theories are better than strong ones, for the strong ones are bound to be wrong. My view is just the opposite: the stronger, the better, for, on the one hand, a correct theory will be strong and, on the other hand, an incorrect one is much more quickly discovered to be incorrect if it is strong than if it is weak.

Our testable conclusion concerns choices in the following situation:

$$
\begin{array}{cc}
 & \begin{array}{cc} \text{I} & \text{II} \end{array} \\
\begin{array}{c} \alpha \\ \bar{\alpha} \end{array} & \begin{bmatrix} a & b \\ d & c \end{bmatrix}
\end{array}
$$

The subject selects a column, the event α selects the row, and the payoff is the corresponding sum of money. On the assumption that $a > b > c > d$, it is evident that if α is an event which never occurs, the subject should never choose column I; whereas if α is certain to occur, then he should always choose column I. Thus, as the probability of α occurring changes from 0 to 1, the probability of choosing column I should also go from 0 to 1. Judging by the data shown in Figure 1 and from related results in other parts of psychology, one might expect this to be a continuous change. Not so, if the decomposition theory is correct. It must be a step function of the sort shown in Figure 2. Just how many steps to expect or where to find them is not specified by the theory, but it says that the function is not continuous.

Obviously, it will be possible to confirm this prediction only if the steps are large and conspicuous. Taking the risk that they might not be, Elizabeth Shipley and I (27) ran the experiment. We used six different payoff matrices for each subject and 15 closely spaced events whose probabilities were known

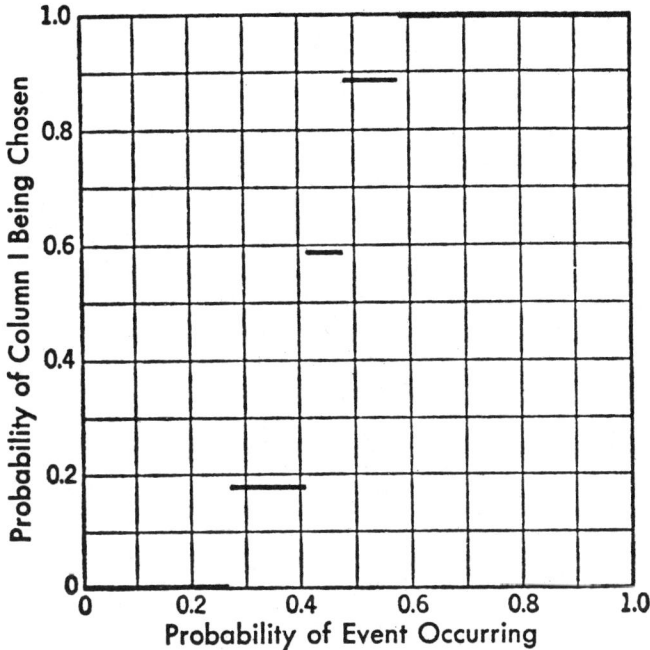

FIG. 2. A typical example of the prediction of the decomposition theory that the choice probability is a step function of the event probability. This figure is reproduced from Luce (24) by permission of John Wiley & Sons.

to the subjects. The events were located in the region where the choice probability changed from 0 to 1. We made 50 observations for each event-payoff condition. Of our five subjects, two exhibited almost perfectly discontinuous functions, and so were consistent with the prediction, but not in a very interesting way. The other three subjects yielded the data shown in Figure 3. You will note that there are curious plateaus of a sort not found in, say, psychophysical data. To see whether these results might have arisen from sampling fluctuations, we fit the data as best we could with smooth S-shaped curves (logistic functions). Assuming that these continuous functions described the probabilities involved, we carried out Monte Carlo computer runs which mimicked the experimental runs. The question was how often in a set of 200 Monte Carlo runs did a

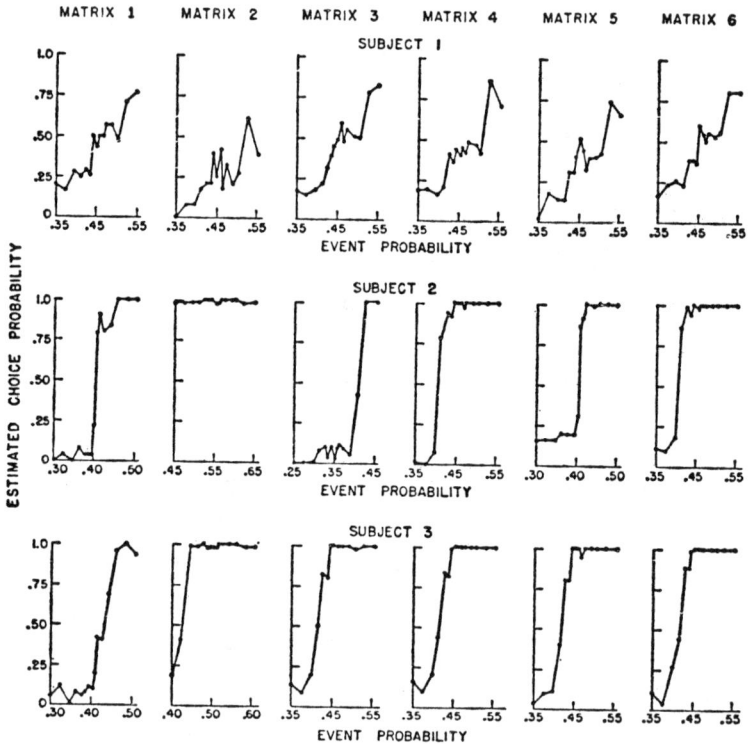

FIG. 3. Estimated choice probabilities as a function of event probability for six payoff matrices and three subjects (Luce and Shipley [27]).

pattern of reversals occur that was at least as marked as that exhibited by the data. It turned out that such patterns were very rare indeed. As a result, we concluded that the data could not have arisen from such smooth probability functions. Whether this means that the decomposition theory is approximately correct is another matter; I am not prepared to argue that it is until we have more studies which confirm it.

LEARNING THEORIES

Our third group of theorists who study human choice behavior when the alternatives are risky have, like the preference theorists, assumed that responses are stochastically controlled. But rather than seek out relations among the response probabilities in related choice situations, learning theorists have focused upon the mechanisms whereby these choice probabilities change with repeated experience in one situation. Without entering into the mathematical details of the learning models,[2] two of their most important features can be mentioned. First, they all describe an organism with an extremely limited memory. This means that they are totally incapable of accounting for human learning of, for example, periodic binary sequences. Second, the learning models assume that when a subject makes a response and it is rewarded, his probability for making that response again is increased a little bit and that when he makes one and it is unrewarded or punished, the probability is decreased a little.

Naïve as these postulates may seem, some data suggest that they are not always grievously incorrect. Suppose, for example, that on each trial a subject must predict which of two lights will appear, the one being correct a random 75 per cent of the time and the other only 25 per cent. Depending on just what specific model one assumes, the subject's asymptotic response probability is predicted to be the same or nearly the same as the event probability of 0.75. A rational analysis says that, to maximize the number of correct predictions, he should always select the 0.75 light. The data, even after hundreds of trials, indicate that human subjects overshoot the event probability but that, in general, they fail to adopt the rational solution.

Or consider another kind of experiment. On each trial, a faint light increment may or may not be presented in a background patch of light, and the subject reports whether or not he thinks it is there. Following his response, he is told whether or not he was correct, and he wins or loses money according to a given payoff schedule. Suppose that there are sensory discrimination thresholds such that internal fluctuations cause the patch to exceed the threshold with one probability, whereas the increment in the patch exceeds it with another, somewhat larger probability. Moreover, suppose not only that the subject

[2] The details can be found in Bush and Mosteller (4) and Bush and Estes (3).

bases his responses on what he thinks he sees but that he biases what he says in terms of the payoff matrix used. Then it can be shown that a maximization of expected utility leads to just one of three possible modes of behavior (Luce [25]). Either on all trials he says no increment is present, or he always says it is present, or he simply reports what he detects. Which

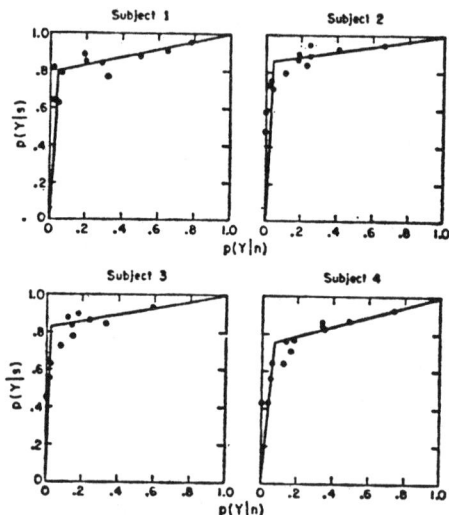

FIG. 4. Plots of the estimated conditional probability of detection response when a signal is presented versus conditional probability of detection response when no signal is presented. The data points were generated by using the same visual signal and background but different payoff matrices (Swets, Tanner, and Birdsall [33]), and the theoretical curves are those of a threshold theory (Luce [25]).

he does depends on the proportion of trials having increments present and on the exact payoffs used. In contrast, if we suppose that the subject learns to bias his responses as a result of the information feedback, then all the intermediate points on the straight lines connecting the above three points are possible. This prediction is shown as the theoretical lines in Figure 4. The actual value of the response probabilities depends on the payoffs and frequency of stimulus presentations. Of these two models, the learning one is favored, judging by the data shown in Figure 4.

I should add, however, that if we assume a different psychophysical model, such as the signal detection model in which there are no thresholds, then the maximization of expected value may yield sensible results. For expositions of this approach, see Green (21), Licklider (23), and Tanner and Swets (34).

Both the guessing and the threshold analyses suggest that a simple adaptive learning process is not, in general, consistent with an optimizing model. This seems, indeed, to be a general proposition. So far as I know, no one has yet stated a learning process which, when the behavior stabilizes at its asymptotic values, results in optimal choices. If, instead of trying to find mechanisms that lead to optimizing behavior, we look for ones leading to the stochastic preference models, the relations are more complex. Suppes (32) has shown that an existing linear learning model, due originally to Estes (18), predicts that the choice axiom holds asymptotically, although it may not hold during the learning phase itself. On the other hand, there do not seem to be any indications that the learning models lead asymptotically to the decomposition axiom. Probably this is related to their failure to lead to a maximization of expected utility, for the decomposition axiom and the expected utility decomposition are certainly very similar in spirit.

CONCLUDING REMARKS

These, then, are some of the main outlines of experimental and theoretical psychological research on the question of choices among risky alternatives. Much the most dominant theoretical ideas have been the subjective expected utility hypothesis and the notion that a person chooses optimally relative to his utility function. Although I cannot cite an unambiguous experimental refutation of these utility notions, their a priori flexibility, coupled with the failure to achieve really smashing experimental successes by using them, leads me to feel that other formulations must be seriously considered.

Of these, we examined two. Both postulate stochastic choice mechanisms. Preference theory is concerned with static constraints existing among the choice probabilities in different, but related, choice situations. Learning theory is concerned with the dynamic constraints relating the choice probabilities on successive exposures to the same choice situation. Ultimately, we must find a way to fuse these two approaches into a single model, specializations of which lead to the restricted theories we are now trying to develop. At present, however, we are far from that ideal state. Our learning models, which have received some experimental support, are not able to account for all our static assumptions, which also have received some experimental support. Moreover, there are some simple learning situations, e.g., prediction of simple periodic sequences, for which the learning models are completely inadequate.

It is not difficult to indicate where some of the trouble lies, but it is quite another matter to recast the models in such a way as to overcome it. Human beings appear to be both "adaptive" and "cognitive"; they sometimes adjust their behavior gradually to experience, and they sometimes "understand" and analyze choice situations. Furthermore, both processes often seem to go on at the same time. The current learning theories are exclusively adaptive, whereas, almost by definition, the static assumptions of the preference theories are cognitive. By appropriately designing our experiments so as to draw upon just one of these two aspects of behavior, we are able to find support for each class of models. But other experiments in which both processes occur can also be designed, and these are bound to reject both classes of models. Such studies are interesting beyond being mere demonstrations, for it is from them that we shall begin to understand which features of a choice situation control the degree to which the behavior is adaptive or cognitive. Only when we develop such insights, will we be able to construct models that effectively take both into account.

If I am not mistaken, students of business have been much more deeply influenced by those theories that are primarily cognitive, especially those in which the decision maker is supposed to behave optimally. At best, this is only a part of what goes on, and certainly in some situations adaptive models are much more to the point. Regrettably, we cannot yet begin even to indicate what differentiates the two classes of situations or to suggest how to synthesize the two classes of models. It is certain, however, that these problems will receive a good deal of attention in the near future, and, judging by the rapid developments during the past decade, we may have a much clearer idea about the relations between these two aspects of behavior in another ten years.

REFERENCES

1. ADAMS, E. W. "Survey of Bernoullian Utility Theory." In H. SOLOMON (ed.), *Mathematical Thinking in the Measurement of Behavior*, pp. 151–268. Glencoe, Ill.: Free Press, 1960.

2. BLOCK, H. D., and MARSCHAK, J. "Random Orderings and Stochastic Theories of Responses," in I. OLKIN *et al* (eds.), *Contributions to Probability and Statistics*, pp. 97–132. Stanford: Stanford University Press, 1960.

3. BUSH, R. R., and ESTES, W. K. (eds.). *Studies in Mathematical Learning Theory.* Stanford: Stanford University Press, 1959.

4. BUSH, R. R., and MOSTELLER, F. *Stochastic Models for Learning.* New York: John Wiley & Sons, 1955.

5. CHIPMAN, J. S. "Stochastic Choice and Subjective Probability," in D. WILLNER (ed.), *Decisions, Values, and Groups*, Vol. I, pp. 70–95. New York: Pergamon Press, 1960.

6. COOMBS, C. H. "On the Use of Inconsistency of Preferences in Psychological Measurement," *Journal of Experimental Psychology*, Vol. LV (1958), pp. 1–7.

7. COOMBS, C. H., and PRUITT, D. G. "Components of Risk in Decision Making: Probability and Variance Preferences," *Journal of Experimental Psychology*, Vol. LX (1960), pp. 265–77.

8. DAVIDSON, D., and MARSCHAK, J. "Experimental Tests of a Stochastic Decision Theory," in C. W. CHURCHMAN and P. RATOOSH (eds.), *Measurement: Definitions and Theory*, pp. 233–69. New York: John Wiley & Sons, 1959.

9. DAVIDSON, D., and SUPPES, P. "A Finitistic Axiomatization of Subjective Probability and Utility," *Econometrica*, Vol. XXIV (1956), pp. 264–75.

10. DAVIDSON, D., SUPPES, P., and SIEGEL, S. *Decision Making.* Stanford: Stanford University Press, 1957.

11. EDWARDS, W. "Probability-Preferences in Gambling," *American Journal of Psychology*, Vol. LXVI (1953), pp. 349–64.

12. ———. "Probability Preferences among Bets with Differing Expected Values," *ibid.*, Vol. LXVII (1954), pp. 56–67.

13. ———. "The Reliability of Probability Preferences," *ibid.*, pp. 68–95.

14. ———. "Variance Preferences in Gambling," *ibid.*, pp. 441–52.

15. ———. "The Theory of Decision Making," *Psychological Bulletin*, Vol. LI (1954), pp. 380–417.

16. ———. "The Prediction of Decisions among Bets," *Journal of Experimental Psychology*, Vol. LI (1955), pp. 201–14.

17. ———. "Behavioral Decision Theory," in *Annual Review of Psychology*, pp. 473–98. Palo Alto, Calif.: Annual Reviews, Inc., 1961.

18. ESTES, W. K. "Toward a Statistical Theory of Learning," *Psychological Review*, Vol. LVII (1950), pp. 94–107.

19. FINETTI, B. DE. "La prevision: ses lois logiques, ses sources subjectives," *Annales de l'Institut Henri Poincaré*, Vol. VII (1937), pp. 1–68.

20. ———. "Recent Suggestions for the Reconciliations of Theories of Probability," in *Proceedings of the Second Berkeley Symposium on Mathematical Statistics and Probability*. Berkeley, Calif.: University of California Press, 1951.

21. GREEN, D. "Psychoacoustics and Detection Theory," *Journal of the Acoustical Society of America*, Vol. XXXII (1960), pp. 1189–1203.

22. GRISWOLD, B., and LUCE, R. D. "Choices among Uncertain Outcomes: A Test of the Decomposition, Transitivity, and Strong Stochastic Transitivity Assumptions," *American Journal of Psychology*, in press, 1961.

23. LICKLIDER, J. C. R. "Three Auditory Theories," in S. KOCH (ed.), *Psychology: A Study of a Science*, Vol. I, pp. 41–144. New York: McGraw-Hill Book Co., 1959.

24. LUCE, R. D. *Individual Choice Behavior.* New York: John Wiley & Sons, 1959.

25. ———. "A Threshold Theory for Simple Detection and Recognition Experiments." Department of Psychology Memorandum MP-12. University of Pennsylvania, 1961. Mimeographed.

26. LUCE, R. D., and RAIFFA, H. *Games and Decisions.* New York: John Wiley & Sons, 1957.

27. LUCE, R. D., and SHIPLEY, E. "Preference Probability between Gambles as a Step Function of Event Probability," *Journal of Experimental Psychology*, in press, 1961.

28. MARSCHAK, J. "Binary-Choice Constraints and Random Utility Indicators," in K. ARROW, S. KARLIN, and P. SUPPES (eds.), *Mathe-*

matical Methods in the Social Sciences, 1959, pp. 312–29. Stanford: Stanford University Press, 1960.

29. MOSTELLER, F., and NOGEE, P. "An Experimental Measurement of Utility," *Journal of Political Economy,* Vol. LIX (1951), pp. 371–404.

30. RAMSEY, F. P. *The Foundations of Mathematics and Other Logical Essays.* New York: Harcourt, Brace & Co., 1931.

31. SAVAGE, L. J. *The Foundations of Statistics.* New York: John Wiley & Sons, 1954.

32. SUPPES, P. *Behavioristic Foundations of Utility.* Technical Rept. No. 23, Institute for Mathematical Studies in Social Sciences, Stanford University, 1959.

33. SWETS, J. A., TANNER, W. P., JR., and BIRDSELL, T. G. *The Evidence for a Decision-Making Theory of Visual Detection.* Technical Rept. No. 40, Engineering Research Institute, University of Michigan, 1955.

34. TANNER, W. P., JR., and SWETS, J. A. "A Decision-Making Theory of Visual Detection," *Psychological Review,* Vol. LXI (1954), pp. 401–9.

35. VON NEUMANN, J., and MORGENSTERN, O. *Theory of Games and Economic Behavior.* Princeton: Princeton University Press, 1947.

6

THE CONCEPT OF POWER AND THE CONCEPT OF MAN

Mason Haire

It is a fad just now to have social scientists working on the problems of business. I will address myself to the question, "Why should this be so?" I suggest that it is *not* just because the Ford Foundation thinks it a good idea, although that makes it much easier. I think it is *not* simply because there is a growing interest both in studies of business and in the social sciences in some common problems like the structure of groups, communication, and the like, although these provide a fertile ground for the interaction. I think it is *not* because of the developing theory and method in the social sciences, although these two developments go a long way toward making the interaction possible. It seems to me that the reason for including the social sciences in the study of business is because the problems of the industrial organization and the setting in which they occur are changing. This change in the social context of business is making the social sciences an integral and necessary part of any considerations of business. I want to speak particularly about two of these changes—the changing concept of power and the changing concept of man. In these two broad areas it seems to me that society's view has changed —and changed in such a way that we can no longer look at business in the narrow sense that we once did. In speaking about these things, I shall deal primarily with organization theory because it is a convenient framework for seeing the impact of these changes on the study of business. However, a variety of other specific aspects of the business problem would serve the purpose equally well.

THE CHANGING CONCEPT OF POWER

Where is authority ultimately grounded? Why do people do what they are told? It seems to me that the answer to these questions in the industrial organization shows a series of steps over a long historical period, all of them tied together as part of a progressive internalization of the seat of power. Let us ask the questions in "classical" organization theory. When I use "classical" in this sense, I mean the kind of theory of organization that we have been used to in the recent past (from, say, Chester Barnard's *Functions of the Executive*). In this kind of system the ultimate seat of authority is clearly outside the corporation. Authority, in the last analysis, is grounded in ownership. It is legitimatized and vested temporarily in the chief executive officer through the medium of the board of directors representing the stockholders. The answer to the question "Why do people do what they are told?" in this system is that they do it because the "or else" means essentially "get off my property."

This position of the owners as the ultimate source of authority has not always been true in the past and is not likely to be true in the future. For a long historical period—we might roughly indicate the period from the Roman Empire to the Industrial Revolution—the ultimate authority of the manager of a business was grounded not in ownership but in the state. For example, Toynbee points out, in *Management's Mission in a New Society*, that the geographical conquests of the Roman armies faced the government with a real dilemma. With the rudimentary administrative machinery of a peasant state, Rome controlled almost all the shores of the Mediterranean. It solved this problem by turning over to private business enterprise every possible branch of public activity—the collection of customs duties, the operation of the farm economy in captured territories, the operation of confiscated mines, and the provisioning of Roman armies. The *authority* with which all this was carried out was still the authority of the state. The *authority* for all the normal business functions—hiring and firing, and the setting of prices and fees, insuring against business risks—came from the state; the *operation* was in the hands of the businessman. This separation of the authority grounded well outside the business activity and the operation inside it is the important characteristic of this period.

It was not only in the Roman Empire that this kind of thing was true. The British East India Company is an outstanding example of the same sort of thing. The operation of privateers with letters patent from the American Revolution through the Civil War fits the same pattern. In some senses the subsidized growth of the railroads and communications industry in the United States continued the trend.

I place the change to the primacy of the owner roughly at the

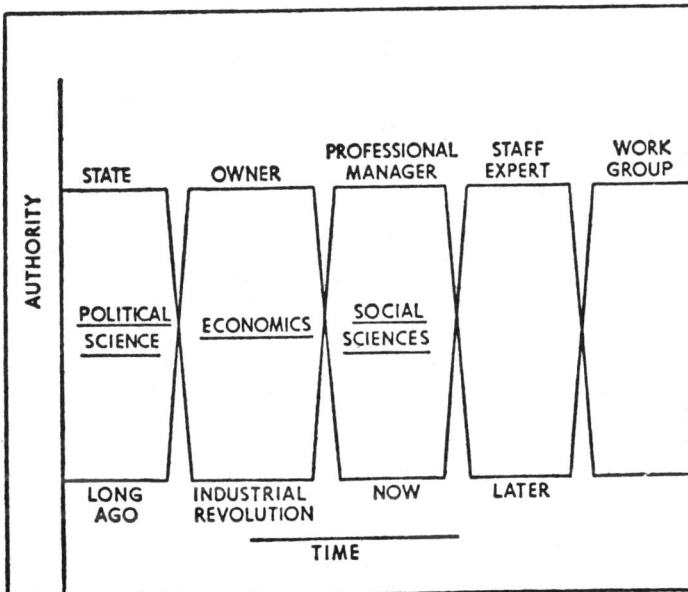

FIG. 1. The rise and fall of power in industrial organizations.

time of the Industrial Revolution. It may well be because the technological change at the time made property, plants, and machinery more and more important and made the formation of concentrated capital the crux of the problem. Before that time, in the simple, dispersed industrial operation, capital was not as important as the protection and approval of the state. At about the same time we see the rise of the rights of property both as a source of authority for the industrial manager and as a general source of value for the community. That well-known social philosopher, Alfred Doolittle, in *My Fair Lady* (and in George Bernard Shaw's *Pygmalion*), speaks of the rights of property as the ultimate prop of middle-class morality, and, indeed, this probably has been true for something over one hundred years as both a social principle and an industrial one.

Today it is reasonable to say that our society is shifting from a success-oriented culture to adjustment-oriented culture. We worry about the teen-ager's psyche and how he fits in with his fellows; he responds by not worrying about property rights, and vandalism is rife. When he breaks all the windows in a schoolhouse and throws paint on the walls, his parents and our schools and our courts do not worry so much about the property as they do about his adjustment. The physical damage is unfortunate, but in an affluent society this does not matter as much as the fact that he is mixed up.

In the industrial organization the parallel to this shift from success to adjustment as a characteristic of the culture (or from property rights to individual rights) is a shift from a conception of executive authority grounded in ownership to one of the same authority which is grounded inside the organization in the process of managing itself. We hear more and more phrases like "the imperatives of the science of management," "the logic of the situation," and "the principles of management." Now, much more than before, when we ask "Why do people do what they are told?" I think the answer is that they either see or have faith that what they are told to do is in fact the appropriate thing to do. This represents a real shift in the ultimate source of authority; in the first place, it is an internalization of the ground on which it is based, and, in the second place, it bases authority on the dynamics of social interaction and the process of management rather than property rights. The internalization has been a progressive thing: when the manager's authority derived from the prince, its ultimate basis was farthest from the corporation; as it shifted to the owner, it came closer to the corporation itself, although it was still outside it; the newer development marks the first time that the ultimate source of authority may be said to have moved inside the corporation itself.

A group of identifiable developments seems to me to have taken place that have made possible this change—from ownership to management—in the answer to the question "Why do people do what they are told?" One of them is the very nature of corporate ownership. The corporation has become very largely divorced from the stockholder-owner and from the financial control of the community in which it operates. The very much more widespread ownership of common stock has made the "owner" of a corporation more impersonal and unidentifiable than ever before. As far as the normal operations of management go, the stockholders' meetings or, indeed, the board of directors' meeting has very little to say. While it is a little extreme, it is perhaps not too much to say that there is no reason, in the operation of the modern corporation, to believe that equity entitles one to any voice in management. Most company presidents, while reluctant to avow this philosophy explicitly in public, operate on this basis in fact. The separation of the corporation from the financial control of the community is equally dramatic. It arises largely out of the growing tendency to finance expansion and diversification out of retained earnings and out of depreciation reserves. This development has cut the corporation loose from the traditional check of the community—from the idea that the corporation has to go to the money market, where the community can exercise its approval or disapproval by furnishing or withholding funds. Both these developments—cutting the corporation off from the owners and cutting the corporation off from the community—

have served to internalize and make autonomous the values by which management operates and to divorce the corporation further from the traditional values that flow from property rights.

A second major development that contributes to this change is the growth of the professional manager. The professional manager is not an owner-manager. Management is once more separated from equity. More than that, the term "professional" means that he has a different orientation in seeking for approval. The professional tends to find approval for his activities among his professional colleagues, among the professional specialists of whom he feels himself to be a member. In this case, he tends to operate, not the way the owner thinks he ought to operate, but the way professional managers approve of operating. Not only is the process of management cut off from ownership, but the value and virtues inherent in the process of management itself are reinforced by the approval of a group of professional managers. A third thing that helped to contribute this change, I think, has been our experience with the tight labor market since the war. It was easy, in prewar days, to think that a subordinate did what he was told because, if he did not, he would lose his job. After fifteen years during which subordinates felt that they could get another job just as good around the corner, the force of this "or else" behind a directive diminished sharply. Management began to look for and find other ways to enlist co-operation and direct activities.

I have pointed to three broad steps in the history of the grounding of industrial authority—the prince, the owner, and the professional manager. Now we come to the reason why we started this whole business: "Why should the social sciences be involved in the study of business?" Different academic disciplines seem clearly relevant to each of these three phases. In the first phase—the ascendancy of the state—the general discipline of political science is particularly appropriate. In the second phase—the era of ownership and property rights, where capital formation and the utilization of a somewhat casual labor market were particularly important—the discipline of economics is particularly relevant. In the third phase, where the seat of authority moves inside the organization itself and becomes grounded in the process of dealing with people in the organization, as well as the economic decisions, the disciplines of the social sciences are clearly demanded. Let me make it perfectly clear, at this time, that I do not mean any of these historical steps to be exclusive. That is, the power of the state never entirely disappeared; the role of the owner has not diminished to zero. Similarly, the relevance of the three disciplines is not an either-or proposition. Political science still has a role to play in the study of business, and no amount of emphasis on the social sciences eliminates the consideration of the corporation as an economic unit. However, looking at the other side of the coin, the changes in the context of the business operation do seem to force a consideration of the problems of the social sciences in a way in which they were never demanded in an earlier social economy.

The purpose of this historical description has been to document an argument for the necessity of considering the social sciences in the study of business. While we have the model before us, we may use it, also, for a bit of forecasting. It seems to me that the tendency to internalize the ultimate seat of authority will go on in the corporation and that it will shift farther and farther inside. I suggest that it will be shifted from being grounded in the professional manager and the process of management until it is ultimately grounded in the work group itself. The final source of authority will be the authority of the work group. The final control will be self-control; the self-control will come from the individual's commitment to the organization, and the individual's commitment will come from his integration into the general goals and activities of the organization.[1] Let me point out that this prediction has no necessary political implications. It is not a prediction, in politico-economic terms, of the socialist development, because

---

[1] On this point I am specifically indebted to D. M. McGregor, of the Massachusetts Institute of Technology. On many others I am equally, though less specifically, indebted to him.

it carries with it no necessary implications of the actual owner-ship of the plant. In many countries this kind of development has gone on along with a political revolution and ended in some form of socialism. There seems to be no inherent necessity for the two to go together. It seems to me perfectly possible to maintain the kind of loose democratic form of political govern-ment that we have and still have the authority in hierarchical organizations move essentially to one that is grounded in the work group itself.

Even before this ultimate development of self-control occurs, another shift in the seat of authority may take place. Indeed, it seems to me that to some extent we are already seeing a shift in authority from the professional manager to the staff expert. In many cases the staff expert is getting to be able to couch the problems in such unintelligible esoterica that the manager cannot make a decision. He can hardly understand what the problem is after it gets restated. Once the computer expert has reprogramed the problem for analysis, the kinds of outcome are all decided, and the degrees of freedom that are left to the manager are considerably reduced. A great deal of the decision making went by unnoticed in setting up the program. The same kind of thing has already happened in the restriction that the industrial relations department has put on the manager in terms of the kinds of things he can and cannot do. We may have here a fine coming-to-fruit of the biblical prediction "Blessed are the meek, for they shall inherit the earth," but it seems to me that the staff expert is in the process of usurping a great deal of the authority of the professional manager. Long before the utopian realization of the authority of self-control, the private language and professional mystery of the staff expert seem likely to come between the manager and the proc-ess he is managing.

THE CHANGING CONCEPT OF MAN

A second change is the changing concept of man. This is nowhere so clear as in the outline of the theory of industrial organization. Whenever we try to plan what an organization should be like, it is necessarily based on an implicit concept of man. If we look a little at the outline of a "classical" organization theory and some more modern alternatives, we begin to see the change in the concept of man.

It seems possible to outline the classical organization theory briefly in a series of points:

1. *Classical organization theory is built on a combination accounting and industrial engineering model.* It breaks the total job down "rationally" and assigns the parts neatly to a group of boxes spread about a family tree. It uses a balance system of authority and responsibility. In principle, a certain amount of authority is pumped into each one of the boxes, and along with this goes a responsibility to pump out a certain kind of productivity. This kind of double-entry system of input and output seems to be one of the first essentials.

This neat balance of authority and responsibility has become a very important myth in writings on organization and perhaps deserves an extra word here. It is a principle that is stated in most of the textbooks and loudly avowed by most companies. I have never been able to understand why, or, indeed, to understand exactly what is meant by it. Let me list, briefly, some of my difficulties with it.

a) In no other part of one's life is authority equivalent to responsibility. We all of us have responsibilities that far exceed our authority. A good check on this point is to consider one's responsibility as a parent. I have never seen a parent whose authority in bringing up his children came anywhere near his responsibility. Similarly, our responsibility as citizens and in many other spheres goes well beyond any kind of authority we have. It is interesting to wonder why organization theorists felt that this should suddenly be changed for the industrial operation. I can only conclude that there was some feeling that it was neater to have the two balance out, whatever that means.

b) A situation in which people's responsibilities are precisely and explicitly defined and limited seems to me potentially frightfully expensive. There is no more expensive operation than the situation in which everyone does exactly what he is told to do and no more. The ideal dodge of the system beater is to say "I did exactly what I was responsible for." We always expect people to do more and to assume more responsibility than their job description speaks of; there seems to be no possible way to give them authority commensurate with this.

c) If we were to try to equalize authority and responsibility, it is a complete mystery to me how it would ever be done. What amount of authority is equal to what amount of responsibility? What kinds of units do we use to measure the two commodities? I can see the argument that if we give a person more responsibility, we ought to give him more authority; this kind of quantification makes sense on the surface. But how much authority is "more" authority? Surely, if we want to equate the two, we must be careful to be fairly precise about how much we mean, and yet the units are not at all clear. If a salesman is responsible for a given territory, the balance theory would presume that he had a given amount of authority. If transportation and communication facilities make it possible for him to cover twice the territory, he has a bigger responsibility. I am not sure that he has twice the responsibility; the geographical units or the dollar volume units may not be good measures of responsibility. But, with this increased responsibility, how do we estimate how much more authority to give him in order to keep the two equal? He has the authority to spend a little more on his expense account. But surely that is not the kind of authority or at least not the only kind of authority that we meant to keep equivalent to his responsibility. Alongside his responsibility, his expense account is a picayune authority. I simply do not understand how this calculus is to be made.

d) The myth of a balanced authority and responsibility seems to me to be in conflict with some other characteristic myths in the classical organization theory. We like to say that the line has the responsibility for producing and selling the product; the staff is there to advise and support and provide expert assistance to the line in this function. A line has the authority. The staff has no authority except within its own staff groups. But, if we maintain the balance of authority and responsibility, this would seem to mean that the staff, lacking authority, has no responsibility! What a comfortable position for the staff man! Can we really say at the same time that the authority is in the line and that authority and responsibility are equivalent?

2. A close second essential characteristic is that the classical *organization theory maximizes neatness and control*. This system of breaking up the job into little pieces and putting them into appropriate boxes at least gives the impression that one knows exactly what ought to be done everywhere, and the balance system of authority and responsibility means that we always have an overview of the output for which a box is responsible. This gives us something we can storm about all the way down through the organization whenever something goes wrong.

3. In line with this emphasis on neatness and control, *classical organization theory puts special emphasis on error* and particularly on the detection of error and its correction *after it has happened*. The standard organization is set up so that everyone has something he ought to do, and, as soon as he does not do it, we find out about it,· give him hell, and see that it gets done. Described this way it sounds ideal; we might, in passing, consider the other possibility—that is, a system which made it less likely that the error would occur in the first place. This kind of detection and correction of error is closely associated with the emphasis on neatness and control. It gives us a kind of system where any boss can go home at the end of the day feeling, "Well, we got through another day without anything going seriously wrong, or at least I caught it as soon as it did." It is probably worth noticing in passing that this value in the organization system is one of the most important for the

adjustment of the executive. It assuages his anxieties about his own adequacy and about the kind of job he is doing. He always has a check to be sure that, contrary to what he was afraid of, nothing has gone seriously wrong. It does not provide the symmetrical check as to whether anything serious has gone right.

4. *This approach to the organization is the classical embodiment of the "extra pair of hands" concept.* The total job is understood only at the top or at the level of the corporate staff. At that level it is clear that more than one man will have to be involved in doing it. Consequently, the pieces are broken up, and an extra pair of hands is recruited for each appropriate little piece and is given the appropriate responsibility and the authority with which to do it. He is not necessarily given much of anything else—that is, much information about why he ought to do it or much feedback about how it is going, unless it is going poorly.

5. In designing the job and in picking these "extra pairs of hands," *classical organization theory assumes man to be relatively homogeneous and relatively unmodifiable.* That is, except for minor differences in abilities and training, which we will take advantage of in selection and assignment, we assume that all people are pretty much alike and that they are going to stay the way they are. Relatively little emphasis needs to be put on the growth and development of the individual.

6. As a matter of fact, very much growth or development in the individual will upset the system. He was put into a job that was an appropriate size for him. If he grows much bigger, he will either want to reach out and do more, which will upset the apple cart, or he will work only about half speed, which has deleterious effects upon his and others morale. Consequently, *another tenet of classical organization theory is that the stability of the employees is a goal.* This means stability not only in the sense of minimizing turnover but stability in the sense of minimizing change within the employees.

7. It is clear from these points that the *classical organization theory is, in its essential character, centralized.* This centralization is necessary for the original planning that parceled out the jobs for the extra pair of hands, is continuously necessary for the error control which runs through the entire system.

8. *The integration of the system is achieved through the authority and control of the central mechanism.*

This last point about integration is a particularly important one, and I should like to digress for a moment from listing the characteristics of organization to discuss this. When we examine an organization, we tend to ask what it is built to do, but we often overlook the most fundamental thing that it is built to do—it is built to hold the organization together. The strongest force that seems to threaten the continued existence of any organization is the persistent centrifugal force that is constantly tending to make it fly apart in all directions at once. This force arises from the fact that the organization is made up of a group of individuals. Whenever an individual joins a group, he gives up some of his individual freedoms, some of his individual goals, and some of his individual satisfactions. This seems to be an inevitable consequence of joining any sort of group, from the marriage partnership up to the largest and most complex corporation or, indeed, a national or international organization. The reason he is willing to do this, presumably, is that, in return for the freedoms and satisfactions that he gave up, he gets some satisfactions as a result of his membership in the group that he would not be able to get otherwise. This contract is always an uneasy one, however. He is still an individual, and he still has individual goals, and there is a constant tendency for him to follow his individual goals at the expense of the group goals. This means that there is a constant tendency for all the individuals in the organization to fly off in the directions determined by their own goals, rather than to move ahead with the singleness of purpose of the group goal. Consequently, one of the most important functions of the organization is to maintain the integration that keeps the individuals together and keeps them (more or less) working toward the single goal of the group.

Two very important consequences flow from this: In the first place, one of the first characteristics of the organization's structure ought to be building it in such a way that it will be maximally resistant to this destructive centrifugal force—that is, that it will tend to hang together. In the second place, one of the primary responsibilities of the chief executive officer is simply to hold the group together. Indeed, most corporations will run pretty well for a long time without much direction. Their direction is pretty well laid down in the general nature of the business and in the things that they have been doing and the equipment they have to do them with. If nobody made any high-level policy, it probably would be quite a while before we noticed it. On the other hand, if nobody kept the parts from flying off in their own directions, we should probably notice it right away. This is the reason why such a large part of the executive's time is spent in running around and pasting the organization back together and tying up discordant and divergent parts in what seems on the surface to be an irrelevant activity but is in fact probably the most important one. As we look at this threat of disintegration, we should remember that the integration in a classical organization theory is primarily achieved through the centralized processes of authority and control. We shall come back to them later in more detail.

Here, then, is a group of characteristics that seem to me to describe the traditional approach to organization. Already we have seen some of the implicit assumptions about the nature of man. Let us look at them in a little more detail. What kind of man would fit well in this system? What kind of assumptions can we safely make about the large body of the labor force from which we must draw all the people to go into the organization, from the lowest hourly paid levels up to, but not including, our own? That is, what are people like? Other people than ourselves, that is.

I think this approach to organization theory is based on the notion that other people (but not I) are, unfortunately, lazy. That is, they will not do anything unless they have to, and consequently we had better build a system that sees to it that they have to do it. This assumption that people are lazy is one of the most crucial and one of the most universal assumptions underlying organization theory. It is the assumption that people will not do anything unless they have to, that they really do not like to work, and that passivity is the essential nature of man. It is from this notion that the idea arises that the system must be thoroughly equipped both with the carrot and the prod. We must design a system with an incentive to hang just before the person's nose and a goad to stimulate him to action whenever he stops. Both of these—the carrot and the prod—are operated from outside the person. The system leaves little room for initiative arising inside the person. The assumption leaves little room for any idea of self-starting. It is often dignified with the elaborate phrase of "The Law of Least Effort." It takes no account of the considerable effort expended in the do-it-yourself movement. A serious question seems to me to be proposed by the man who does exactly what he is told on the job and no more and then goes home and sweats blood building a boat in a bottle or putting a new patio on the side of his house.

Further than that, and equally unfortunately, people are shortsighted. Not only will they not do anything unless they have to, but they will not see that it ought to be done. We better add that to the system—build in a mechanism that will make sure that they know from moment to moment what ought to be done. There is no real need to let them know beyond the moment to moment; that would only confuse them.

This is partly because it is, also unfortunately, generally true that people are not interested in the company when they are on the job. (We must keep remembering that this is people other than ourselves.) Not only are they lazy and shortsighted, but they are selfish. Consequently, we build a system in which they do what they are told, rather than rely on their seeing what ought to be done in the company's interest and doing it.

People are quite apt to make mistakes, and we had better build a system that will allow for that.

People (again other people, that is) have poor judgment, if any. Since this is unfortunately so, we had better build a system that gives them a minimum of judgmental discretion. Ideally, we shall need a program that tells them what to do all the time, since they do not know and cannot foresee the factors involved.

Finally, and so unfortunate that perhaps we ought not to mention it, there is sometimes a suspicion that people may even be a little dishonest basically.

These are the implicit assumptions about man which classical organization theory seems to me to be based: He is lazy, shortsighted, selfish, liable to make mistakes, has poor judgment, and may even be a little dishonest. With this kind of building material, it is no wonder that we do not come up with much in the way of organization.

Now let us try another view of the nature of man. Let us assume that he has the same basic drives as the next fellow. The trick is to build and operate an organization that will elicit and use them.

His shortsightedness may come from the fact that information has been withheld from him for one reason or another. Maybe we can overcome some of that.

He may well make mistakes—if so, many of them are probably part of a reaching-out for new behaviors, and, as such, we had better be careful not to sit on them too hard. Innovation and growth come from this; error will still have to be watched closely.

He needs more information to make better judgments. Further than that, his personal commitments to the organization and its objectives will greatly influence the goodness of his judgment.

Even his honesty (whether it is putting his hand directly in the till or soldiering on the job or padding his expense account) is probably largely a function of his integration into the organization and his commitment to it. Now we are making a quite different set of assumptions about the basic nature of people. There is a surprising tendency to consider other people as having quite different characteristics from oneself. Table 1

TABLE 1

ATTITUDES TOWARD OTHER'S SATISFACTIONS

What Subordinates Want in a Job Compared to Their Superiors' Estimates

	As Men:	As Foremen: Men		As General Foremen: Foremen	
	Rated Selves	Would Rate	Rated Selves	Would Rate	Rated Selves
Economic Variables:					
Steady work-steady wages...	61%	79%	62%	86%	52%
High wages...............	28	61	17	58	11
Pensions and security.......	13	17	12	29	15
Not to work too hard.......	13	30	4	25	2
Human Satisfaction Variables:					
Get along with people......	36	17	39	22	43
Get along with superior.....	28	14	28	15	24
To do good quality work....	16	11	18	13	27
To do interesting work......	22	12	38	14	43
Chance for promotion.......	25	23	42	24	47
Good working conditions....	21	19	18	4	11
Total..............	*	*	*	*	*
Number of Cases.....2499		196	196	45	45

Source: Copyright © 1961 by McGraw-Hill Book Co., Inc. Used by permission of Rensis Likert and McGraw-Hill.
* Percentages total over 100 because they include three rankings for each person.

shows some interesting data presented by Likert in his recent book, *Organization Theory.* In this situation workers were asked to rate how important various things were to them on the job. Their foremen were then asked to make the same rating in the way they thought the men would make it and then to make the rating for themselves. Then the general foremen were asked to make the rating the way they thought the foremen would do it and then to make the rating for themselves. The foremen rated steady work and high wages as important variables for the men (79 per cent and 61 per cent). On the other hand, they thought that they were much less important for themselves (62 and 28 per cent). On the other hand, the general foremen thought that the foremen would rate these variables much higher (86 and 58 per cent). For themselves the general foremen only rated them 52 and 11 per cent. All the way across, each group thought these were very important for their subordinates but not for themselves. The same kind of pattern shows up in the variable "not working too hard." Each superior thought it important for his subordinate; each person thought it not very important for himself. The other side of the coin shows up in the value that is placed on getting along with other people and getting along with a superior. In each case the superiors thought that these were not very important to the subordinates; in each case everyone thought that these were important to themselves. When we think about the kinds of people for whom we have to build an organization, we tend to have a very pessimistic view for everyone except ourselves.

Some similar data appear in an unpublished study done by Professor Lyman Porter at the University of California. A random sample of the American Management Association was asked a series of questions, among them the question "How important is initiative in your job? In your superior's? In your subordinate's?" The data showed answers to these three questions at a variety of levels in the organization. In every case, no matter what the level of the respondent, his job and his superior's demanded initiative. His subordinate's did not. This was true all the way up and down the hierarchical ladder. The man had to have initiative to do his job; the person below him was better off without it.

Suppose we were to build an organization based on the radical assumption that the other people in the organization are not very different from ourselves.

Again, let me list in bare headings a set of the characteristics that seem to me to flow from an organization based on this kind of man.

1. Such an organization would look for not the "extra pair of hands" but for the initiative, innovation, and judgment of the individual.

2. It would be built not on an accounting model but on a group-structure model emphasizing the cohesion and integrity of each unit group and the linkage of each group to the groups above and below it and the groups around it. This "group-structure model" is illustrated in Figure 2. While this picture of an organization chart does not look very much different from the conventional one, it has markedly different implications. Likert uses this description to emphasize the "linking pin" function of the superior at every level. His primary responsibilities are to see that the people below him are indeed a closely knit group

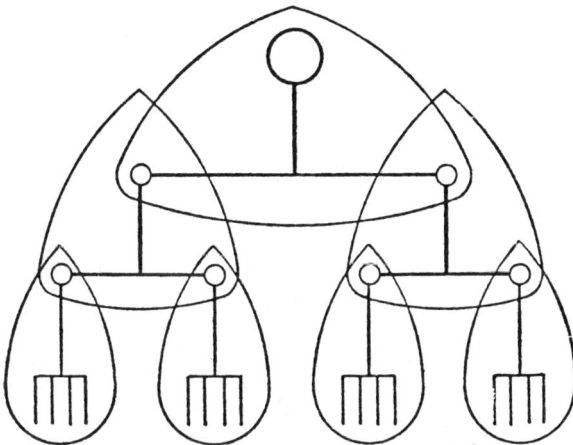

Source: Rensis Likert, "A Motivational Approach to a Modified Theory of Organization and Management," in Mason Haire (ed.), *Modern Organization Theory* (New York: John Wiley & Sons, Inc., 1959), p. 193.

FIG. 2. Group-structure model of an organization.

(indicated by the triangle), to see that he is a member of that group, and to be a member of the group formed by the people at his level and the person above him. In this sense he is a member of the group below and the group above, he is the "linking pin" between the two. This emphasis on the group membership in two directions is important. It also means, with respect to authority and influence, that the superior's capacity to influence his subordinates depends on his capacity to influence his own superiors.

3. It would maximize participation.

4. In seeking initiative, it creates an atmosphere in which there is freedom to make mistakes. This does *not* maximize error. It is the situation we hope to create for a child growing up, in which he is free to try

things, to learn, to grow, and to develop without someone looking over his shoulder all the time, expecting him to fail. I repeat that this does not involve a lower standard of quality or more error, but it does involve an atmosphere that places a real reliance on the other person. It is worth pointing out here that, just as the control of error in the classical system is a protection to the adjustment of the executive, this freedom to make mistakes may well be adjustmentally threatening to the executive. We need to ask, then, how much of the organization's drive we can afford to spend in order to protect the executive's adjustment.

5. Such an organization would assume man not only to have initiative but to be highly modifiable. Both training and leadership in general would encourage him to change, develop, and learn.

6. Integration in such a system is obtained through mutual confidence and trust, shared objectives, commitment, and both social and job skills appropriate to these structures and objectives of the organization.

7. This kind of organization is, in its essential nature, decentralized.

8. The growth and development of the employees is a primary goal of such an approach.

Now we have a very different kind of organization. What kinds of things will we have to do differently? Let me list just a few of the outstanding ones briefly:

1. Probably the first and most important thing will be giving up the use of financial data for punitive control. A typical system now is for an executive to have periodic financial reports on the operations of the divisions under him. In general, he usually employs these reports to hit his subordinates over the head when things are not going well or to hold over their heads like a threatening club just in case they slip. We generally collect financial data on operations (budget data) and production data and forward them to higher levels of the organization which can use them as a means for tight control over their subordinate group. In principle, as far as management goes, these data should probably be reported at the level of the group which generates them. This group would then report them on up to the next level, where they could be discussed in terms of the degree in which they met the shared objectives which had originally been set, in terms of the problems encountered in accomplishing these objectives, and the like. When this is accomplished for the managerial process, it should still be possible to forward such data to higher levels for planning purposes. The purpose of the exercise is to avoid using this information for punitive control.

2. The next big thing that would have to be changed would probably be the neat job descriptions. Such descriptions are typically set up to tell a man exactly what he should do and exactly where his bailiwick ends. They are designed to eliminate conflict in the system. An al-

ternative approach to the organization might well be to permit over-lapping and conflict in areas of responsibility, hoping to encourage the initiative and to utilize the conflict rather than to smother it.

3. The next big thing that would be challenged would be the concept of "information appropriate to the level." All three of these tie together —the broad job description and total responsibility, using operating information for shared objectives rather than punitive controls, and the sharing of information. Typically, we have hoarded information to pro-tect the status of each level from those beneath it. The approach I speak of would suggest that the information appropriate to any level is all the information. Current technological developments in the com-munication process present a real alternative in this dimension. As elec-tronic data processing develops, we have the clear alternative of using the greater speed either to centralize more information or to collect information so rapidly that it can be decentralized efficiently. Which choice we take seems to be of crucial importance to the concept of organization and the concept of management. A good example of the extreme use of technological advance in the centralization of the man-agerial process was reported in the newspapers at the time of the Little Rock integration crisis. When National Guard troops were sent in, a closed-circuit television and radio system connected the Pentagon di-rectly with the field. This made it possible for the commanding general to look over his subordinate's shoulder even at the range of a thousand miles, to second-guess every decision, and to say, "Now do this— Oops! you did it wrong—now do the other thing." The kind of subordi-nate leadership that this kind of operation is apt to develop is ap-palling.

4. In order to make this concept of organization work, some very creative rethinking of compensation is necessary. It is not perfectly clear how it would work, but two lines of approach seem to me ap-parent: Our present approach, from the philosophy of job evaluation, is to state exactly what a person is supposed to do, assess its difficulty, its danger, its arduousness, its skill, and the like, and then pay him in return for these things. The pay, to the person, is an asset balancing the liabilities of the work. A very different spirit is entailed when we consider the possibility of paying a person, not in return for the un-pleasant thing he has just done, but in order to make it possible for him to do all he can. I might suggest that that seems to be the model on which university compensation is based. Research workers tend to be paid, not on a piecework basis, but in order to make it possible for them to work creatively. A second influence in the compensation philosophy comes from rewarding specific work accomplished and not from the function of making it possible to accomplish it. Let me cite an example from another sphere. Our basketball coach at the University of California was noted for building teams rather than prima donnas (and very successful teams, too!). One of the things he insisted on was a change in the system for awarding letters. Traditionally, in order to get a letter, a man had to play sixty minutes during the season. The

coach insisted that a Senior who had been working with the team through his college career, had kept himself in condition, in practice, and ready to play deserved a letter. The reward, he insisted, should go not for making baskets but for making it possible to make baskets. The shift in emphasis from the reward for individual accomplishment to the reward for contributing to team potential is an important one. We often overlook the same kinds of reward in industry. For example, we usually insist that one of the functions of the supervisor is to train people to assume leadership positions, and yet there are very few cases in which this kind of effort on the part of the supervisor is rewarded. We tend to reward or punish in terms of the number widgets produced. They are so much easier to measure. It does not matter that their ultimate production may rest on subtler criteria. Our compensation scheme typically overlooks the constructive variables and pays off for individual accomplishment.

Here we see a little bit of the influence of concepts of man on the forms of organization. When we look at the problem of organization, we seem to be answering the question, "What is the best way to organize?" In fact, we are answering the question, "Given the way I believe people to be, what is the best way to organize?" We usually do not question the first part of that— "What I believe people to be." It is clear that there are very widely different answers to the question of organization, depending on the implicit assumptions about the nature of human nature. I have the strong feeling that assumptions about human nature are in the process of shifting from the former to the latter these days and that, with this shift in the assumptions, the shape of the organization is also changing. I think that the change in our thinking has gone further with respect to the concept of man than it has with respect to the philosophy of organization, although that is following, too. It seems to me that one sees little bits and pieces of changes in organization that are flowing unwittingly from changes in the concept of man and that the wave of the future is going to be this kind of organization. While we anticipate this change in the organization of the future, it is worth pointing out that it is quite apt to have a tremendous competitive advantage attached to it. Operating with an outmoded organization—or with an organization that implies a concept of man which employees are unwilling to accept for themselves—may well put a firm at a decided disadvantage vis-à-vis a competitor whose thinking is more in tune with the kinds of things that the members of his organization are ready to accept.

One might ask "Is this 'nothing but' human relations warmed over?" I think not. In its pure form the human relations movement seems to ask for increased satisfactions for members of the work force because they were a good thing in themselves— that is, that one *ought* to provide more satisfactions for people. This approach suggests:

1. That there is more impetus and initiative to be derived in an organization based on a concept of man that is clearly different from the fundament of classical organization theory.

2. That there is a competitive advantage in a concept of man that is acceptable to the society and the labor force from which organization members are drawn.

3. That a concept of authority that is acceptable to the society is closely related to the forms of organization and the conception of man and, importantly, to the continued existence of corporate entities in the sense that we know them.

TITLES IN THIS SERIES